# THE CPS STORY:
## *An Illustrated History of Civilian Public Service*

# THE CPS STORY:
## An Illustrated History of Civilian Public Service

## Albert N. Keim

Good Books

Intercourse, PA 17534

# Acknowledgments

## Photo Credits

Cover: top left and lower right—Swarthmore Peace Collection; top right—"MCC Collection," Archives of the Mennonite Church; lower left—Mennonite Historical Library and Archives, Bethel College.
Richard Reinhold, 7, 25; UPI/Bettmann, 9; G.P. Putnam's Sons, 11; Menno Simons Historical Library, Eastern Mennonite College, 14; Canadian Mennonite Bible College Publications, 12; MacMillan Publishing Company, 13; Bruce Comly French, 19; Herald Press, 20, 23; Geraldine Z. Glick, 22; "MCC Collection," Archives of the Mennonite Church, 27, 33, 37, 51, 66, 67, 71, 70, 74, 80, 93, 113 (top), 115 (top), 117 (top), 118 (top), 119 (bottom), 121 (bottom), 124 (bottom); U.S. Military Institute, Carlisle Barracks, Pennsylvania, 29; University of North Carolina Press, 30; Swarthmore Peace Collection, 31, 39, 40, 41, 42, 44, 45, 47, 48, 52, 53, 54, 55, 58, 60, 61, 63, 69, 73 76, 77, 78, 82, 83, 84, 85, 86, 87, 88, 90, 91, 92, 95, 111, 112 (both), 113 (bottom), 114 (both), 116 (both), 117 (bottom), 121 (top), 122 (bottom), 123; Mennonite Central Committee, 35; Mennonite Historical Library and Archives, Bethel College, 50, 56, 64, 65, 89, 92, 96, 115 (top), 118 (bottom), 119 (top), 120, 122 (top), 124 (top); Mennonite Historical Library, Goshen College, 62; Brethren Archives, 94.

Litany of the War Resister's League—Swarthmore Peace Collection Civilian Public Service Camps list (p. 109)—NSBRO, *Directory of Civilian Public Service* (© 1947).

Design by Dawn J. Ranck

THE CPS STORY: AN ILLUSTRATED HISTORY OF CIVILIAN PUBLIC SERVICE

Copyright © 1990 by Good Books, Intercourse, Pennsylvania 17534
International Standard Book Number: 1-56148-002-9
Library of Congress Card Catalog Number: 90-71118

Library of Congress Cataloging-in-Publication Data

Keim, Albert N.
    The CPS story : an illustrated history of civilian public service
/ Albert N. Keim.
            p.        cm.
    Includes bibliographical references.
    ISBN 1-56148-002-9 : $11.95
    1. World War, 1939-1945--Conscientious objectors. 2. Historic
peace churches--United States--History--20th century.
    3. Conscientious objectors--United States--History--20th century.
    I. Title
D810.C82K45    1990
940.53'162--dc20
                                                90-71118
                                                CIP

# Table of Contents

# 1

# No Room
# for COs

John Yoder finally realized the war was over when he topped the hill and saw the farm spread out below, an oasis of peace in a world which had known only war and violence for six years. The farm seemed unchanged since his departure four years before. The world had changed, however, and so had he. Four years ago he had been a simple farm boy. He was no longer that, but he was not sure he could tell in what ways he had changed, who he had become.

The train carrying him to Hill City, South Dakota, in 1942 had been crowded with noisy young men in military uniforms. His civilian clothes confirmed his draft orders—he was a conscientious objector, a CO. His destination was a Civilian Public Service camp.

*An idyllic and peaceful Mennonite farm in Lancaster County, Pennsylvania, during the war-torn 1940s.*

CPS #57 was a work camp for conscientious objectors who refused to participate in World War II.

John remembered his feelings of fear and awe as he carried his suitcase from coach to coach in search of a seat. That train had been an alien world which he had never encountered before. The isolated quiet farm had not prepared him for his four-year adventure in Civilian Public Service.

He was not an accidental conscientious objector. He had been taught, and believed in a fuzzy sort of way, that war and violence were against the spirit and purpose of God. The church community to which John belonged was not just objecting to this war; his people had objected to and refused to serve in any war for 400 years. Their objection was seldom expressed in rhetorical moral terms. Instead, for them it was a collision of two communities: the prevailing society which claimed to manage the world, whose failure seemed to often erupt in war, and the little community of Mennonite Christians intent on putting into practice the words of Jesus in the Sermon on the Mount. It was the clash of those two communities, both claiming complete loyalty from John, which had put him on the train to Hill City, South Dakota. John had chosen the alternative program of his faith community.

## The "Good War"

World War II was not an easy war for COs. It carried none of the ambiguity of the Vietnam War. It was, as Studs Terkel has put it, the "Good War," a clear case of good versus evil, freedom versus tyranny. On what possible basis could one choose not to fight against Hitler and the evil he represented? It was a hard call for many pacifists and most elected to fight the Nazis.

Of 34,506,923 men who registered for the draft during World War II, only 72,354 applied for conscientious objector status. Of those, 25,000 accepted noncombatant service in the army; that is, they were soldiers who agreed to work in the Medical Corps or in any military work which did not involve actual combat. Another 27,000 failed to pass the basic physical health examination.

A total of 6,086 were imprisoned for their refusal to participate in any form of service whatsoever. Of those, 4,441 were Jehovah's Witnesses whose refusal was based primarily on their claim of ministerial exemption. Beyond the Jehovah's Witnesses, only 1,645 persons refused any of the alternative provisions of the law.

Just 12,000 conscientious objectors chose the only other alternative available: to engage in "work of national importance" under civilian direction, the Civilian Public Service program.

The number of conscientious objectors in World War II was

**Litany of the War Resister's League used at many peace rallies during the 1930s:**

*"If war comes, I will not fight."*

*"If war comes, I will not enlist."*

*"If war comes, I will not be conscripted."*

*"If war comes, I will do nothing to support it."*

*"If war comes, I will do everything to oppose it."*

*"So help me God."*

exceedingly small. One might have expected far more, for a powerful pacifist movement had developed in the 1930s, with hundreds of thousands of adherents. The pacifists had vowed to oppose war as a means of solving international disputes by refusing to do military service. Thus, when war came in 1939, many military planners and politicians assumed they would face major problems in recruiting soldiers. They expected large numbers of conscientious objectors. As it turned out their fears were largely unfounded. Most of the vocal pacifists of the 1930s disappeared when the war began, and the expected wave of conscientious objectors never materialized.

But even small numbers of conscientious objectors can cause problems for governments at war. During World War I there were fewer than 2,000 absolute conscientious objectors, but they created big headaches for the American army. The conscription law had recognized religious conscientious objection to war, but left to the President and the War Department the decision of what to do with the conscientious objectors. As a result, COs were drafted into the

*American infantrymen fighting the German army in Belgium break into a house searching for enemy snipers.*

army and posted to military camps with the hope that many of them would decide to adopt noncombatant service.

## Difficulties During World War I

After inspecting "an interesting group of conscientious objectors" at Camp Meade in Maryland, Secretary of War Newton D. Baker wrote to President Wilson that he had ordered the conscientious objectors to be segregated from their fellow soldiers. He hoped that the feeling of rejection would soon bring them around to cooperation and that only a hard core of Amish and Quakers would be left. Baker's experiment failed. Few COs changed their minds.

For the young conscientious objectors posted at the army bases the biggest problem was deciding how much to cooperate with the base commanders. Was washing the dishes in the camp kitchen cooperating with the military? What about weeding the flower beds? Could one put on a uniform, but refuse to carry a rifle? Many of these men were members of the Historic Peace Churches (a designation which usually includes the Mennonite Church, the Amish, the Hutterites, the Quakers and the Church of the Brethren). President Woodrow Wilson's government underestimated the tenacity of these Historic Peace Church (HPC) conscientious objectors. The military had little patience with the so-called "conchies." Refusing to follow orders, these men often suffered shortened rations, solitary confinement, physical abuse and many court-martials.

Brethren Elder D. A. Crist visited Camp Funston, Kansas, in October 1917, and reported that "three [men] were put in separate rooms today with but one blanket (no heat in the rooms at all), and are to be given nothing to eat but bread and water until they obey orders."

The experiences of four conscientious objectors highlighted the situation of COs in the army camps. The four were drafted and assigned to Camp Lewis in the state of Washington. Upon arrival at camp they refused to participate in any camp activities. After a court-martial, the men were sentenced to 20 years at hard labor and sent to Alcatraz. Wrote David Hofer, one of the young men:

> When we arrived we were placed down in a sub-basement, very dark, filthy, and alive with vermin. We were undressed and a uniform laid out. Those who placed us there said: "You'll die here. We took four out of here dead yesterday." We were kept four and a half days without food, and with only half a glass of water every 24 hours. We slept on the cement floor without cover. For the last 36 hours in the "hole" our hands were chained to bars in the door, drawn up so high that our feet barely touched the floor. We were struck across the arms with knotted lashes so

that when we came out, we could not put on our coats.

After several months the men were transferred to Fort Leavenworth Kansas, where two of them died as a result of the mistreatment.

Such experiences made a deep impression on the Historic Peace Churches, and as war clouds appeared on the horizon in the 1930s, the three main HPCs—Mennonites, Church of the Brethren and Friends—engaged in an intensive search for a solution for COs during wartime. They considered several options.

One alternative was noncombatancy, rejected because it contributed directly to the war effort. Some pacifists had been willing to

*Reclamation of forestry services. . .*
*Relief and reconstruction work in local communities*
*Medical and health services*
*Farm service*

*Signers: Rufus Jones and Walter Woodward, Friends; E.L. Harshbarger, Harold S. Bender and P.C. Hiebert, Mennonites; Rufus D. Bowman and Paul H. Bowman, Church of the Brethren*

*Rufus Jones was the pioneer Quaker leader for CO concerns during World War I.*

*A group of Russian Mennonite COs in the forestry service just prior to World War I.*

serve in the Signal Corps or Medical Corps. Others had served in quartermaster and other noncombat units. The assumption of many military persons was that COs rejected actual killing but accepted the necessity of noncombatant activity in wartime. This was a basic presumption of War Department policy during World War I.

Rufus Jones, venerable Quaker peace spokesman during the First World War, exasperated by the War Department's refusal to concede to Peace Church rejection of noncombatancy, commented grimly, "It apparently did not occur to the Washington people that objection was anything more than an objection to the direct killing of people. They do not seem to understand that we are opposed to the military system . . ."

A third alternative service model came from the Mennonite conscientious objector experience in Russia. When Tzarist Russia imposed universal military conscription in the 1870s, Mennonites were able, after great difficulty, to create an alternative service for their young men known as the Mennonite Forestry Service. Their task was the reforestation of southern Russia; their length of service was the same as the military. The men worked out of base camps operated by the Mennonite church, but the work was supervised by

the chief forester in each district. The church paid all living and maintenance expenses. The men received a nominal wage from the government. The program lasted 35 years, but the massive dislocations of World War I eventually destroyed the program.

*An AFSC ambulance unit: the experience of this relief service in France during and after World War I served as one model for World War II alternative service.*

By the mid-1930s ominous events abroad portended war. Hitler passed the Nurnburg Laws and repudiated the Versailles Treaty. Mussolini invaded Ethiopia. Japan was poised to continue its invasion of China. The dictators were on the march.

Alarmed by world events, the Historic Peace Churches, under the leadership of Mennonite editor H.P. Krehbiel of Kansas, held a three-day conference at Newton, Kansas, in October, 1935. Nearly 80 persons from the three denominations were present. The group appointed a three-person committee—Orie Miller, Mennonite; C. Ray Keim, Brethren; and Robert Balderston, Friend, to coordinate Peace Church preparation in case of war.

Earlier in the year, Mennonites meeting at Goshen (IN) College devoted an entire conference to a discussion of appropriate action by COs in wartime. A paper by Guy Hershberger asked the question, "Is Alternative Service Desirable or Possible?" The young Goshen College professor answered his own question with a strong yes. He cited both the Russian Mennonite Forestry Service and the Quaker

Service during and after World War I as examples of attractive alternative service possibilities.

A second option was absolute noncooperation. This might mean refusal to register, refusal to appear for induction, or any of a series of actions whose end would be prosecution and, almost certainly, imprisonment. Its radical idealism was also its chief drawback: not many 18- or 20-year-olds had the maturity or moral stamina to carry it out.

By the mid-1930s a loose consensus among COs emerged around the idea of a form of alternative humanitarian service in lieu of military service. The alternative service idea was attractive to many Peace Church people because, as loyal citizens, they wanted a way to discharge their citizen obligations in wartime. Citizenship required more than sitting out a war in prison, for example. Alternative service, they believed, was more desirable than prison as a witness against war; it offered a practical demonstration of how to behave in wartime. Through alternative service they were sure that COs would gain moral authority to witness against war and the passions generated by the war.

*These men presented a letter and a statement of Historic Peace Church goals to President Roosevelt on January 10, 1940.*
*Left to Right: Clarence Pickett, Walter Woodward, Rufus Jones, P.C. Hiebert, H.S. Bender, Rufus Bowman and Paul H Bowman (missing — E.L. Harshberger).*

Dan West, Brethren peace enthusiast and organizer, argued for a "relief machine which would engage 'in nonpartisan relief in wartime.' We can earn the right to ask for exemption from military duty if we get busy. Our record will be a better argument than our intentions, however sincere, without that record."

## An Active Witness Against War

Alternative service came to be seen as a kind of CO "moral equivalent" of war. The models the HPCs drew on came from World War I experiences of the Quakers; from the work-camp ideas of Swiss Quaker Pierre Ceresole during the 1920s; and from the late 19th, early 20th century experience of the Mennonites in Russia.

During and immediately after World War I the American Friends Service Committee (AFSC) was able to place several hundred relief workers in France. The workers rebuilt war-devastated housing, restored farmland for crop use and provided medical service to war-sufferers. The COs worked close to the battlefield and had an opportunity to directly help the victims of the war. It was a dramatic example of a "moral equivalent" to war.

Pierre Ceresole, a Swiss pacifist, was impressed by the work of the Friends in WWI. He invented the work-camp movement, which became popular in the period between the two world wars. The purpose of the work camp was to bring young people together for manual labor on humanitarian projects. Equally important was the opportunity these young people had to discuss the great issues of peace, war and justice while working together. The onset of fascism gave such encounters practical relevance. The combination of voluntary service and constructive conversation had great impact on many of the hundreds of thousands of young people involved in work camps.

Alternative service, he argued, should be under civilian direction; the work should be morally important and challenging enough so that the blandishments of wartime patriotism could be deflected by young CO idealists. Alternative service should be, as American Friends Service Committee's Clarence Picket put it, the "moral equivalent of war."

The Church of the Brethren developed a detailed alternative service plan in 1938. With it they included a list of types of service "not consistent with the historic position of the church," such as military chaplaincy, YMCA work with soldiers, military hospital work, Red Cross work under military auspices and any forms of military service.

The Church of the Brethren took the lead in preparing a paper entitled "Our Group Procedure in a War Crisis." The paper urged the HPCs to "plan together, to work together, and if necessary to suffer together."

The period between the World Wars was a productive one for the peace churches. They did learn to work together, so that when military conscription began in 1940, they were able to present a common front and a working consensus about how they wanted their conscientious objectors treated under the new draft laws.

# 2

# Legislating a Policy for Conscientious Objectors

The German army invaded Poland in the early fall of 1939. In the spring of 1940 they overran Scandinavia and the Low Countries. By June 1940 they occupied Paris. The first phase of the European war which would become World War II was over. England was clearly the first target in the next stage of the War. In the United States the argument raged: should the United States come to the defense of Britain? Isolationists argued that the United States had no business getting involved in another European war: "Let the Europeans settle their own problems." President Roosevelt was eager to help Britain.

But 1940 was a presidential election year. The party presidential conventions loomed just ahead. With isolationist feeling running so strongly, the President, hoping for reelection to an unprecedented third term, had to tread carefully as he tried to prepare for a war he was sure the United States would become involved in.

Roosevelt was appalled by the poor condition of the American military. The army had only 200,000 men armed with World War I weapons. The Air Force was almost nonexistent. The Navy rode on World War I vintage ships. Upgrading the military was a high priority on the President's agenda.

In May 1940 he asked for $2.5 billion to begin rebuilding. Congress voted the appropriations. Given the isolationist sentiment in Congress, the President was surprised at his success. But he also knew there were limits. Building up military manpower was his most politically dangerous problem. Few people in the country would support drafting American young men for another American expeditionary force to fight a war in Europe. To suggest such a course, Roosevelt knew, was political dynamite. At a news conference on May 28 Roosevelt stressed arms and equipment. "We are not talking about a draft system, either to draft men, women, or money, or all three," he said.

Roosevelt was a realist. He knew there was little chance of enacting a military draft in peacetime. Furthermore, the armed services didn't want a draft law. The Joint Army and Navy Committee responsible for military manpower recruiting had adopted the "Civilian Volunteer Plan." Under that program each state governor would direct an aggressive volunteer recruitment effort to raise necessary manpower in the event of a national emergency. The assumption by all concerned was that conscription would only be possible after a declaration of war.

Thus, at the end of May 1940, neither the President nor the military contemplated or sought the enactment of a conscription law. Yet within three weeks such a bill would be introduced in Congress, and within four months a conscription law would be in place, 15 months before the United States declared war. How could such a thing happen?

## Inadequate Provision for COs in Draft Bill

New York lawyer Grenville Clark was a member of the Military Training Camps Association, (MTCA) a World War I veterans group which believed the United States should get into the war quickly and help roll back the Nazis. They believed a draft was urgently needed. So they wrote a draft bill, and Grenville Clark took the proposal to Washington. The military opposed the idea, so Clark went directly to the President. Roosevelt refused to support the bill, but he did concede to Clark's suggestion that he appoint MTCA member Henry Stimson, a Republican, as Secretary of War. Stimson then arranged to have the MTCA-written conscription bill submitted to Congress as the Burke-Wadsworth (after the Senate and House sponsors) Bill. On June 20, 1940, the day the Germans invaded Paris, Congress began its consideration of the draft bill.

The proposed bill had a CO clause almost identical to the World War I law. It read:

> Section 7(d): Nothing contained in this Act shall be construed to require or compel any person to be subject to training or service in a combatant capacity in the land or naval forces who is found to be a member of any well recognized sect whose creed or principles forbid its members to participate in war in any form, if the conscientious holding of such belief by such person shall be established under such regulations as the President may prescribe; but no such person shall be relieved from training or service in such capacity as the President may declare to be noncombatant.

The bill repeated the mistake of World War I: it assumed that most Historic Peace Church COs would serve in noncombatant military service. Clearly they would not. Furthermore, the phrase "member of a well recognized sect whose creed or principles forbid its members to participate in war in any form" overlooked or excluded general religious or non-religious COs. Dismayed HPC leaders feared the nightmare experience of World War I was about to be replayed.

## The COs Respond

The Central Committee of the Friends General Conference met at Cape May, New Jersey, in early July 1940. They wrote a strong statement opposing the bill and sent Paul C. French to Washington to testify on their behalf at a Senate Committee hearing on July 9.

*Paul Comly French was a birthright Friend who had worked many years as a reporter. Just prior to 1940 he served as director of the Federal Writer Project. So he knew Washington well, and had excellent contacts. He knew who the real decision-makers were and how to influence their actions.*

*During 1939 he wrote* We Won't Murder, *an analysis of the CO experience in World War I. His conclusion: ". . . the best method of handling conscientious objectors to war becomes one of unconditional and unqualified exemption from all conscription for either military or so-called alternative civilian service."*

*The book and his government experience made him uniquely qualified for his next job. During the summer of 1940 he led the HPC effort to modify the Burk-Wadsworth conscription bill to include an alternative service provision. In the fall he became the executive secretary of the newly formed National Service Board for Religious Objectors, the agency created to manage CPS. He continued as executive secretary throughout the war.*

*In 1940 Orie Miller was executive secretary of Mennonite Central Committee. He was also the Mennonite member of the Continuation Committee of the Historic Peace Churches. Later in 1940 he became the vice-chairman of the newly formed National Service Board for Religious Objectors. Since he was also a member of nearly every church-wide committee in the Mennonite church, he was in a position to give overall administrative direction to the Mennonite CPS program.*

*In some ways a cautious man, he had an unusual ability to put idea into organizational form and shape. His close relationships with M.R. Zigler, Paul Furnas, Harold Bender and other Peace Church leaders oiled the gears of the cumbersome CPS organization and, against great odds, made it work.*

His instructions were to work to defeat the bill.

Within two weeks it became apparent that defeating the bill was out of the question. French was placed on the payroll of the Friends War Problems Committee and became the coordinator of the Friends, Mennonite and Brethren effort to modify the bill to meet their special concerns.

Agreeing that the bill required modification, the Historic Peace Churches took the initiative. At the behest of the War Problems Committee, Friends lawyer Harold Evans drafted an amendment to the bill requesting the following:

1. A register of conscientious objectors.
2. A civilian bureau for conscientious objectors reporting to the Attorney General.
3. Provision for COs to do work of national importance under civilian control.

4. A national board of appeal.

5. A complete exemption for conscientious objectors who refused all service.

French delivered the amendment to the Senate Military Affairs Committee. Only two members voted for it.

Undaunted, French gained permission from Deputy Chief of Staff General Shedd to discuss the matter with Colonel Victor J. O'Kelliher, who was the officer in the War Department managing conscription legislation. O'Kelliher agreed to discuss the matter and, after some compromises, agreed to four of the clauses. The fifth request, which called for complete exemption for absolutists, was rejected by the Colonel.

During review of the new material by General Shedd and several Military Affairs Committee senators, a phrase was inserted exempting objectors who came to their conviction because of "religious training and belief." The intent was clearly to limit the scope of conscientious objectors, an idea much regretted by the churchmen.

Despite that, on the next day, July 25, French carried the revised amendment to the House Military Affairs Committee, which agreed to incorporate it into the House version of the Bill. Forty-three witnesses testified on behalf of the CO clauses in the bill during the House Committee hearings in late July.

In August the Bill was debated in the House and Senate, and slowly the CO clause, so carefully constructed in July, began to change form. The most unfortunate change was to take registration and hearing procedures out of the Justice Department and place them in the hands of local draft boards. This meant that COs would be at the mercy of local draft boards who were often more keen on patriotic duty than civil justice. It was a major setback.

A second implication of this change also became apparent. By placing registration and appeals in the hands of draft boards, the management of all CO matters would be handled by the new Selective Service Administration, an organization meant to conscript men for military service and owned and operated by the military system. As in World War I the military would again control the fate of COs. French, bitterly disappointed, remarked sadly, "It is curious how a few minutes can undo the work of a month or more."

## No Legislative Support

The failure of the Historic Peace Churches to get their most important provisions into the conscription bill was the result of one dramatic fact: not one Congressperson or Senator took up their cause. This stood in contrast to Britain where many members of Parliament took strong positions in favor of CO rights. The British had a progressive program for their COs during World War II.

The only government advocates for the CO provisions were the manpower recruiters in the newly formed Selective Service organization. Their goal was to make sure COs would not be a serious problem when conscription began. To accomplish that they tried to do two things: keep the number of COs as small as possible (the new "religious training and belief" clause inserted into the bill's section 7(d) served that purpose) and handle inducted COs efficiently and unobtrusively.

As Congress debated the Burke-Wadsworth Bill during August, HPC leaders spent many days in Washington lobbying legislators

*M.R. Zigler became the coordinating center of the CPS program in the fall of 1940, when he was elected the first chair of the National Service Board for Religious Objectors. He thus served as Paul Comly French's immediate superior. In 1941 he became executive secretary of the Brethren Service Committee, and thus assumed general oversight of the Brethren CPS program.*

*Zigler brought a wonderful zest and verve to all of his work. The risk-taking and experimentation which characterized the creation of CPS was partially a result of his leadership. He was a lifelong advocate of interdenominational cooperation, and CPS offered him a wonderful opportunity to put those convictions into practice.*

*M.R. Zigler and Orie
Miller worked together to
keep the CPS vision alive.*

and officials, and consulting with each other on the issues. They
provided Paul French advice and counsel. A great sense of common
purpose emerges as one reads the record of events of this historic
summer of 1940.

The Friends, because of experience and disposition (they believed in intervention in government policy as an integral part of
their witness), took the lead in the effort. The Mennonites and
Brethren were grateful for their leadership. Wrote Orie Miller for the
Mennonites, ''[We] must give the Quakers credit for having carried

*During the interwar period Major Lewis Hershey (pictured opposite with "plain" men) served on the Joint Army-Navy Selective Service Committee, working on military manpower issues. With the formation of the Selective Service System in 1940, he was first assistant to the director of Selective Service, and then became director. For the next 29 years he managed America's draft system.*

*Hershey liked CPS. His goal was to solve the conscientious objector problem with the least amount of trouble. A few vociferous COs could mean big problems for the military. So Hershey was in favor of any program for COs which the public, particularly veterans' groups, would tolerate.*

*Hershey liked the Mennonites. He sometimes called himself the "Mennonite General"; there may have been some Mennonites in his family tree, he thought. The general was very adept at negotiating the conflicting demands of over-heated wartime patriots, on one hand, and the stubborn resistance of conscientious objectors. Ironically, he was one of the few public figures who would speak out on behalf of the COs.*

*Hershey liked the out-of-the-way Civilian Conservation Corps camps*

through the brunt of this. As a church we appreciate this help from the Friends very much."

M. R. Zigler of the Brethren observed, "The Friends are doing a most noble job in organizing the movement to give favorable consideration to the conscientious objector in every way."

Congress passed the draft bill on September 14, 1940. Two days later the President signed the new Selective Training and Service Act. The CO section read:

Section 5(g): Nothing contained in this Act shall be construed to require any person to be subject to combatant training and service in the land and naval forces of the United States who, by reason of religious training and belief, is conscientiously opposed to participation in war in any form.

Any such person claiming such exemption from combatant training and service because of such conscientious objections whose claim is sustained by the local draft board shall, if he is inducted into the land or naval forces under this Act, be assigned to noncombatant service as defined by the President, or shall, if he is found to be conscientiously opposed to participation in such noncombatant service, in lieu of such induction, be assigned to work of national importance under civilian direction.

The new law was an improvement over World War I. The intense work of the HPCs during the summer of 1940 had born fruit. The definition for CO exemption was broadened from sectarian membership to include those who "by reason of religious training and belief" had become conscientious objectors. This meant that Protestant, Catholic and Jewish COs would now be recognized. Unfortunately it excluded secular COs. It recognized COs who could not do noncombatant service by offering work of national importance under civilian direction. The appeal process was lodged in the Justice Department; there would be no court-martials for World War II CO draftees. Cases would be tried in civilian courts.

The Act also created major problems. Local draft boards determined classifications, a nightmare for COs with hostile draft boards. The program was to be run by the Selective Service System whose job was conscripting fighting men, not COs. This was a major disappointment for Peace Church people who had hoped for a civilian administrative system. The Act ignored absolute COs, those who could not participate with the system at all; their only option was prison. And it did not define "work of national importance."

## Putting the Program to Work

With the passage of the Selective Service Act a new phase of Peace Church cooperation began. On September 4, five Mennonites, six Friends, five Brethren and Walter Van Kirk of the Federal Council of Churches met at the Commodore Hotel in Washington to survey the future. They faced big questions.

What form or forms should the "work of national importance" take? Who should operate the program? Should each church group develop its own plan? How would the project be financed? Should the HPCs accept government money?

Paul French was asked to remain in Washington for another 60 days to give leadership during the next months. The Brethren and the Mennonites would each send a representative to join French; the three would function as a committee representing CO concerns. A general meeting was set for October 5 in Chicago to try to design an alternative service program.

It soon became clear that the Peace Churches were running far ahead of the government in developing plans for the CO program. When French, Orie Miller, Warren Bowman and Walter Van Kirk met with General Shedd, manpower chief in the General Staff, they discovered that he had no idea what "work of national importance"

*for the COs. It took a lot of pressure to bring him to agree to humanitarian and social work projects because of their negative public relations potential: putting COs in public places might create problems.*

*He never understood those CPS men who meant their service to be a protest against war. He disliked government-run CPS camps; their potential for trouble was simply too great. After World War II he was a major factor in the decision to avoid a camp system for cold war COs.*

might be. He sent them to an assistant, Colonel Partridge in the manpower section, who was congenial but had no authority to begin planning a program. Partridge sent them to Frederick Osborne, chairman of a new committee established by the President to review all Selective Service regulations. Osborne promised cooperation, but his committee was not authorized to initiate programs.

Finally, they found their way to Colonel Lewis B. Hershey, director of the Joint Army and Navy Selective Service Committee. Hershey's advice was, "Get your groups together and draw up proposals. No one in the government has given much thought to the problem."

On October 1, 1940, Colonel Hershey became Acting Director of Selective Service. The next day he asked Paul French if the Friends would agree to manage the service program for COs. French took the idea to Philadelphia the next day where the Friends War Problems Committee agreed to do the job. That evening Ray Newton, American Friends Service Committee Peace Section Secretary, accompanied French to Chicago where they presented the idea to their Mennonite and Brethren colleagues. Newton and French discovered that Dan West of the Brethren had a plan which he called the "Brethren Volunteer Service." And the Mennonites had just that morning decided to endorse a Mennonite church program. It was urgently clear that the Historic Peace Churches needed to begin coordinating their plans.

# 3

# Designing Civilian Public Service

The 65 Peace Church representatives who met in Chicago during October 4 and 5, 1940 were no longer strangers to one another. Many of them had attended the historic Newton, Kansas, peace conference in 1935 and had been working on peace and conscientious objector plans ever since. Now the military conscription of their young men was no longer in the future. A plan had to be designed.

M. R. Zigler of the Church of the Brethren presided at the

*The designers of CPS: M.R. Zigler, Church of the Brethren; Orie O. Miller, Mennonite church; Paul Furnas, Friends; and Arthur Swift.*

meeting. Paul French reported on recent developments in Washington. Out of the subsequent discussions came agreement to create a National Council for Religious Conscientious Objectors, renamed later, National Service Board for Religious Objectors (NSBRO). Eight members representing the three Peace Churches were its governing board. M. R. Zigler was elected chair of the board, with Orie O. Miller as vice chair. Paul French became executive secretary. The new agency was formally established October 11, with the assignment to handle all negotiations with the government on matters relating to conscription.

Its first task was to design an alternative service program. Within a fortnight NSBRO had a plan. A National Board for Civilian Service would administer the program through an executive officer. The executive officer would report to the director of Selective Service. The National Board for Civilian Service would be staffed by HPC members and function as an independent body setting policy for its executive officer.

Alternative service projects would be of two types: one, government-operated to serve non-HPC conscientious objectors; the other under HPC control. A variety of work camp, refugee and relief activities at home and abroad were proposed.

They presented the plan to Clarence Dykstra, who was appointed the new director of Selective Service on October 17, 1940. His assistant, Wayne Coy, and a government review committee spent two days discussing the church plan. On October 29 the committee delivered its version of the proposal to Dr. Dykstra. Their changes were minor and the HPCs accepted the revision.

Dykstra took the plan to President Roosevelt for his consent and was surprised when the President voiced a negative reaction to the alternative service idea. Paul French reported, "The President expressed instant and aggressive opposition to the plan." Work camps were too easy, the President said. COs should be drilled by army officers just like soldiers. The President's hostility came as a shock to everyone. French and Dykstra, wise to the ways of Washington, enlisted the aid of one of the President's assistants, and eventually the President was persuaded that the program had merit and reluctantly endorsed it. But his attitude had a serious effect on plans for funding. Dykstra had misjudged the situation. Getting funds to operate the program would not be easy.

Meeting with the National Council for Religious Conscientious Objectors at the Hotel Harrington, Dykstra and Colonel Hershey reported their dilemma. To ask Congress for funds to operate the program would expose the program to hostile scrutiny and might scuttle the entire project. They also reported that any money appro-

priated could only be used in government-operated camps. Most HPC groups rejected a program run by the government.

So the fateful decision was made — the HPCs would finance the program. Each of the governing bodies of the three Historic Peace Churches endorsed the church funding idea. The normally reserved Orie Miller of the Mennonite Central Committee spoke Mennonite feelings when he promised that Mennonites "would gladly pay their share of the bill. They would do it even though every Mennonite farmer had to mortgage his farm." The Friends' Five Year Meeting in Richmond, Indiana, approved a resolution that if government funds became available they should not be accepted.

It was a rash decision for such normally cautious people. They wanted maximum autonomy, and they believed the best way to get it was to pay their own way. It was also politically smart. No one could accuse them of using government funds to avoid their citizen responsibility to fight for their country. Selective Service heartily approved of the idea; no one could accuse them of being soft on "conchies."

*The device used to operate the fishbowl lottery which called up draftees for service in World War II.*

## Experiment Begins with Little Design

The President signed Executive Order 8675 on February 6, 1941. A unique church-state partnership, known as Civilian Public Service (CPS), was born. It began as a six-month experiment. It lasted through a year of uneasy peace, four years of total war and two years of demobilization.

The program assigned COs to camps for soil conservation and reforestation work. The Agriculture and Interior Departments provided supervision for work projects. The Federal Security Agency made civilian conservation camps available. Camp furnishings came from the War Department. Selective Service paid transportation expenses and supervised the overall program. The cooperating churches financed all other necessary parts of the program, including day-to-day management of the camps, subsistence costs for the camps, and all care and maintenance of the men.

The actual relationship of the religious agencies to Selective Service was vague. Were the churches agents of the Selective Service or were they contractors, carrying out a contractual service? The answer was unclear.

**Maj. Gen. Lewis B. Hershey**

*For an A-1 army*
*In 1-A trim*
*Selective Service*
*Selected him*
*To present free rides*
*To the front and fame,*
*In sort of a glorified*
*Numbers game.*
*You feel a draft?*
*You'd better check.*
*It's That Man*
*    breathing*
*On your neck.*
    *— Ethel Jacobson*

Selective Service was pleased with CPS. When he discussed CPS with the President in December 1940, Clarence Dykstra reminded FDR that "during the World War, conscientious objectors presented difficulties out of proportion to the numbers involved." Creating CPS, he argued, was a way to "avoid so far as possible a recurrence of such difficulties." He also argued for CPS as an experiment to see whether voluntary groups and government could work together in a great "national service."

Dykstra's successor, General Lewis Hershey, once called CPS an "experiment in democracy to find out whether our democracy is big enough to preserve minority rights in a time of national emergency."

Hershey liked CPS for other reasons as well. When Senator Elmer Thomas introduced legislation in 1943 to eliminate the CO clause from the conscription bill (all able-bodied men should serve in combat, the Senator believed), Hershey argued against it. "Do you want to saddle the military with thousands of non-cooperators?" he

*Rustic shelters characterized CPS camps. This one is at Petersham, Mississippi (CPS #9).*

asked. It would be a nightmare. Far better, he said, to put COs in out-of-the-way camps. As he put it, "The CO, by my theory, is best handled if no one hears of him." Besides, continued the General, nearly 10 percent of the COs are being "salvaged" for military service. And COs are working for the national welfare at almost no cost to the American taxpayer. Hershey liked CPS.

The HPCs were uncertain about their relationship to Selective Service; not so Selective Service. Tom Jones, President of Fisk University and first Director of Friends CPS, told of a trip to the Friends camp at Merom, Indiana, in the company of Colonel Louis Kosch, deputy to General Hershey.

As Jones enthusiastically described his hopes for Civilian Public Service, the dour Colonel Kosch cut him off with, "Who do you think you are? Don't you know I'm in charge of these camps under Selective Service?"

Jones replied that he thought the HPCs were promised complete autonomy. "My dear man," said Kosch, "the draft is under United States government operation. Conscientious objectors are draftees just as soldiers are. Their activities are responsible to the government. The Peace Churches are only camp managers."

The direct authority of Selective Service over CPS men was laid out in a famous memo by another Selective Service officer, Lieutenant Colonel McLean, in 1942. Wrote McLean:

> The program is not carried out for the education of an individual, to train groups for foreign service or future activities in the postwar period, or for the furtherance of any particular movement. Assignees can no more expect choice of location or job than can men in the service. From the time an assignee reports to camp until he is finally released he is under the control of the Director of Selective Service.

> He ceases to be a free agent and is accountable for all of his time, in camp and out, 24 hours a day. His movements, actions and conduct are subject to control and regulation.

> He ceases to have certain rights and is granted privileges. These privileges can be restricted or withdrawn without his consent as punishment, during emergency, or as a matter of policy. He may be told when and how to work, what to wear, and where to sleep. He can be required to submit to medical examinations and treatment, and to practice rules of health and sanitation. He may be moved from place to place and from job to job, even to foreign countries, for the convenience of the government regardless of his personal feeling or desires.

When CPS was created in the fall of 1940 such a comprehensive definition of Selective Service authority would not have been accepted by the HPCs. By 1942 it was too late to turn back.

## The Men Come

The first CPS camp opened at Patapsco State Park near Baltimore on May 15, 1941, seven months before Pearl Harbor. It was a Friends-administered camp. A week later a Mennonite camp opened at Grottoes, Virginia, and a Brethren camp began at Lagro, Indiana. Numerous camps were opened in the following months.

The program grew rapidly. By July 1942, there were 3,738 men in CPS: 1,572 in 13 Mennonite camps, 1,035 in 12 Friends camps, 1,048 in 10 Brethren camps. Two Catholic camps had 68 men and a cooperative camp had 15.

When CPS ended in April 1947, 12,000 men had served in its ranks. They had worked in 152 camps, units and projects. Of that number, 5,830 men were in the Mennonite program. In September 1945, Mennonite CPS reached its largest size—4,288 men. The Brethren had 1,353 men in CPS; the Friends 951; all others, 3,862 men.

In that same month in 1945 there were nearly 5,000 COs in prisons in various parts of the country. Absolutist resisters of the draft were extremely unpopular in World War II. One journalist

*CPS #56 located in Waldport, Oregon, was a Brethren camp.*

called the imprisoned COs egomaniacs, psychopaths, eccentrics and saboteurs. Larry Gara, a draft resister, was considered very dangerous because he was believed capable of trying "to collect groups of people to march on public offices." Gara served three years in jail for refusal to register.

Most imprisoned COs were Jehovah's Witnesses. Since draft boards refused to give them a ministerial exemption (all Jehovah's Witnesses consider themselves ministers), more than 4,000 Jehovah's Witnesses went to jail.

Like so many new organizations created to deal with the War, the CPS program simply exploded. One month there was nothing; the next month a maze of organization was in place. The result was confusion and experimentation.

The sense of confusion was partly the fault of the HPCs. Their decision to each operate their own camps created an additional layer of organization. And Selective Service, not wanting to deal with three religious agencies, insisted on the creation of the National Service Board for Religious Objectors (NSBRO) to be a clearinghouse for all CPS matters. There was, finally, Selective Service itself, new and untested. The net effect was many wheels within wheels.

The wonder is that it worked as well as it did. That it succeeded is a tribute to youth, ingenuity, goodwill and the energy generated by conviction.

Selective Service was the ultimate arbiter of all CPS matters. General Lewis Hershey, Director of Selective Service after July 31, 1941, was busy organizing military manpower so he delegated direction of CPS to Colonel Louis Kosch, chief of the Camp Operations Division of Selective Service. The authority of the Camp Operations Division ranged over the whole area of CPS programs. Assisting Kosch was A.S. Imirie, who managed the CPS hospital units. Colonel Franklin McLean and Victor Olsen were fieldmen, visiting CPS camps and filing reports. An array of clerical persons managed the records and papers of the COs. With only two exceptions the staff of the Selective Service Camp Division were army officers, giving the lie to the stipulation that the work of COs was to be "under civilian direction."

The Camp Division had the last word on all matters of importance for CPS. It approved all projects, using as criteria such questions as: "Is the work important to the government?" "Will the CO do the work?" "Will the community tolerate CPSers?" "Will CPSers displace local labor?" The initial location of camps was usually made in response to requests from soil conservation, forestry or related government agencies. Later when work in mental hospitals began, the request for men often came from the hospitals. Robert Kreider, who gave leadership to the Mennonite mental hospital projects, remembers visiting hospitals to determine whether the situation would be appropriate for CPS work. He would then make a recommendation to the appropriate office at NSBRO, which in turn would clear the location with Selective Service.

## The Bureaucracy Takes Shape

All assignments of men had to be ratified by Selective Service, as were transfers, reclassifications and appeals. Selective Service determined hours of work, holidays and furloughs. Detailed monthly reports were made on each man about his time on project, leaves, illnesses, accidents and behavior. These reports were compiled by each camp administration.

Transfers of men were normally a result of a call for volunteers. When a new mental hospital unit opened word would go out to the camp units, and men could ask for a transfer if they had an interest. In some cases the church headquarters staff would tap specific persons for assignments. This was often the case when leadership

*CPS #5 located near Colorado Springs, Colorado, was a Mennonite camp.*

*Members of the board of directors of National Service Board for Religious Objectors. Back row: M.R. Zigler, Orie Miller, Leroy Dakin, Paul Furnas, Arthur Swift. Front: Paul Comly French, Harold Row, Albert Gaeddert.*

positions were being filled from the ranks of CPS men.

At the second level was NSBRO. Its task was to handle CPS matters in Washington for the Peace Churches. Paul C. French served as its executive secretary throughout the war. Its work was unusually difficult, positioned as it was between the Peace Church CPS programs and Selective Service. It grew rapidly in the early months.

Three sections were created to handle the work. The Assignment Section, run by J.N. Weaver, assigned men to the various camps upon notification by the SSS that they had been classified IV-E (conscientious objectors available only for work of national importance) and inducted. During the first eight months of CPS the Section handled 2,200 assignments. The Section also tracked transfers and reassignments.

The Complaint Section, under Huldah Randell, became the advocate unit for COs who were wrongly classified or whose draft boards refused to give them CO status. The Section often received as many as 40 letters a day requesting assistance.

George Reeves managed the Camp Section. Its primary task was selecting camps for CPS and, after approval by Selective Service, arranging with church agencies for their operation. By September 1941, the Camp Section had 18 camps open and running. By 1943 there were nearly 150 CPS units in place. By then many of the units were so-called "detached service," such as mental hospitals, farm service and other special projects.

The Camp Section also managed all government property for CPS, as well as dealing with camp work procedures and a wide variety of liaison activities.

Eventually a Special Projects Section was established to manage mental hospital and farm work projects.

Trying to explain the circle within circle design of the NSBRO sections, a Camp Section wag wrote: "The [Assignment] Section tries to get them into camp, we try to keep track of them once they're there, then the Special Projects Section tries to get them out."

Beginning in 1942 NSBRO published a four page semimonthly newsletter, the *Reporter.* Its purpose was to help communicate information and news important to CPS men. *A Camp Director's Bulletin* carried information of special value to camp directors.

At the third level were the Historic Peace Church CPS directorates. Each church established an administrative organization to manage its CPS program. They directly administered the operation of the camps, appointing the director and his assistants, seeing that camp routines were established, setting up educational, religious and recreational programs. They also disbursed funds to operate the camps, as well as raising funds from their constituencies.

The American Friends Service Committee, located in Philadelphia, established a CPS committee made up of three groups: representatives of the Yearly Meetings of Friends, members selected by the AFSC, and twelve men from Friends CPS camps and units. The executive director of the CPS Committee was Paul Farnas, a veteran of World War I Friends conscientious objector field work.

The Mennonites used their relief agency, Mennonite Central Committee in Akron, Pennsylvania, as the supervisory body for the CPS program. Henry A. Fast of Newton, Kansas, became the first director of Mennonite CPS in November 1940. He had two assistants, one for the western part of the country and another for the east. Given the large number of Mennonite COs, the organizational and management challenge was daunting. Eventually more than 60 persons were located at Akron, Pennsylvania, as administrative and support staff for the CPS program.

The Church of the Brethren placed their CPS program under the Brethren Service Committee, located in Elgin, Illinois. Paul Bowman became the first director of Brethren CPS. His staff managed 14 base camps and dozens of special projects. The Brethren program was particularly challenging administratively because nearly half of the men in their camps and units were other than Brethren. This also posed financial problems, since many of the non-Brethren men lacked adequate financial support-groups to help carry the cost of their maintenance.

## What to Bring to Camp
### *From Instructions Sent To Each Camper*

1. Not more than one suit of clothes suitable for Sunday wear.

2. Not more than one camp suit; these clothes suitable for wear evenings and Saturdays.

3. Overcoat.

4. Raincoat.

5. Work Clothes:
   a. Three pairs of good quality blue denim trousers.
   b. Three good quality work shirts.
   c. Three good quality blue denim jackets.
   d. Light sweater or similar windbreaker garment to wear under jacket when necessary.
   e. Two pairs of gloves.
   f. Two good pairs of work shoes.
   g. One pair of overshoes (arctics).
   h. One warm cap.
   i. Six pairs of work socks.

6. Three shirts for good wear.

7. One pair of good business shoes.

8. Several pairs of Sunday socks.

9. Underwear:
   a. Two pairs medium weight long underwear with long sleeves and legs.
   b. Lighter underwear if desired for camp purposes.

10. Two pairs of pajamas.

11. Linens:
   a. Three bed sheets good quality; at least 63 by 99 inches when finished.
   b. Two pillow cases, same quality material.
   c. Three hand towels.
   d. Two bath towels.
   e. Two wash cloths.

12. Personal items—supplies may later be replenished in camp:
   a. Shaving supplies.
   b. Dental supplies.
   c. Toilet supplies.
   d. Shoe polish supplies.
   e. Stationery and stamps.
   f. Literature supplies—notebook, devotional literature, Bible, etc.
   g. Musical instrument if desired.
   h. Hand mirror.
   i. Mending kit, needles, thread, pins, buttons, etc.
   j. Other personal items, that you consider indispensable.

Do not bring a whole wardrobe, that is too many supplies. They will be a burden to you in camp. This clothing need NOT BE NEW, but can be supplied from your present wardrobe; the above list is to guide you as to quantity and quality.

# 4

# "Work of National Importance"

It was May 15, 1941 and the first Civilian Public Service camp was opening. The first 26 conscientious objectors arrived with 54 reporters and photographers in tow. It was a historic event. The place was an abandoned Civilian Conservation Camp in the Patapsco State Forest near Baltimore, Maryland. Patapsco, also known as CPS #3, was a National Park Service camp directed by the American Friends Service Committee.

By the time Civilian Public Service ended six years later, nearly

*A work crew boards a truck to ride to the "project" at Coshocton, Ohio (CPS #23, AFSC).*

12,000 CPS men had logged over eight million man-days of work for their country. Had the government paid for the work at the army rate as provided by law, it would have spent $22,000,000. Its actual bill was $4,731,000 for administrative expenses. The COs were not paid and their families and churches contributed $7,202,000 for their support.

The CPSers worked at an immense variety of projects, including conservation and forestry camps, hospitals and training schools, university labs, agricultural experiment stations and farms, and as government survey crews. They built roads, fought forest fires, constructed dams, planted trees, built contour strips on farms, served as guinea pigs for medical and scientific research, built sanitary facilities for hookworm-ridden communities and cared for the mentally ill and juvenile delinquents.

*Millions of young men used dynamite in World War II. This CPS man at Coshocton, Ohio, is using it for peaceful purposes: blasting stumps (CPS #23).*

Much of the work was important; some of the results were long lasting. There were long-range benefits from the medical and scientific experiments COs participated in. They demonstrated new non-violent techniques for the treatment and care of mental patients. They brought the appalling conditions in mental hospitals to public attention. But for their work the New Deal soil conservation programs would have been terminated during the War.

There were also many frustrations with make-work and a lot of lost motion. The poet Milton's line "They also serve who only stand and wait" was a popular CPS phrase. In one forest camp the men

*CPS men hamming it up in an old wreck.*

*Smoke jumping, while glamorous, could be hazardous.*

were moving firewood, bucket-brigade style, from a stack in a ravine to a truck 50 feet away on the nearest accessible road. Since there were too many men for a direct line to the truck the forestry foreman ordered them to form a long curved line in order to use all the men. He didn't want any malingering.

Few CPSers could appreciate the logic of digging postholes in frozen ground or the pressure put on some CPS campers to assist farmers who were making large profits from war-inflated farm prices. From the vantage point of an idealistic young conscientious objector, many of the tasks assigned to CPS seemed irritatingly superfluous in a world suffering horribly from global war. Work as basic as conservation or forestry lost its rationale when set in such a scale of values.

How this situation affected the CPSer depended on the meaning he invested in his conscientious objection. If he was merely avoiding involvement in the war, CPS work was often tolerable for him. But if he believed that being a conscientious objector meant actively opposing war, actively working for peace or actively aiding the victims of war, he found the experience often intensely frustrating.

## Forest Service Camps

Probably no assignment carried a greater aura of mystique and adventure than Smoke Jumping. Highly trained crews of CPSers parachuted into rugged country to put out fires. The tactic was highly successful because it meant that most fires were attacked while they were still small and could be put out quickly with minimal manpower.

It was a popular program. More than 300 men volunteered for the assignment when the first group was formed in the early summer of 1943. The Mennonites administered the camp, located 30 miles from Missoula, Montana. Initially 60 men were trained for the project, but by the end of the war 240 men from all HPC groups had served in the program. After training, the men were deployed in small squads at a number of strategically placed base camps in Montana, Idaho and Oregon.

Smoke Jumping was a mixture of extreme tedium and high excitement. Between fires the men chopped wood and made hay. The hay was fed to the pack mules used to carry equipment and supplies. The excitement began when the terse message from a ranger announced a fire. An example was the 1944 Berg Mountain fire.

The ranger's call came into the parachute loft at Hudson near Missoula on Sunday afternoon, August 6. The fire was on Berg Mountain in rugged country near Riggins, Idaho. The area on the

*When given his assignment in the Technical Office, Harold Kaufman was asked "Are you afraid of work?" "No Sir," Harold replied. "I could lie down and sleep right beside it!"*

*CPS men on the Grove Creek Fire.*

map was captioned, "Land of No Return." The dozen or so Smoke Jumpers all hoped to go, but only eight were selected. The rest, in the best Smoke Jumper fashion, waited and prayed for more fires.

Boarding a Ford Trimotor with their gear, they hunkered down for the two hour ride to the fire. Addison Carlson jumped first, then Wilmer Carlsen, followed by the other six. Walt Reimer demolished his chute by stripping it down over a snag. The Trimotor roared overhead dropping tools and supplies, then disappeared over the horizon.

It was six o'clock in the evening. The men were on their own. Their quick arrival meant that the fire was still small, some 300 feet wide and half a mile long. Dividing into two crews they built fire lines along each side of the fire, completing the work by five o'clock the next morning. After four hours of sleep, they began mopping up the fire. Late in the afternoon a wind whipped up the remaining embers of fire, and it was only many hours later, after throwing up new fire lines, that the fire was finally completely throttled.

Tuesday morning the crew hiked out to the nearest road and via truck and plane arrived back at the Missoula camp late that evening.

The Missoula Smoke Jumpers fought 75 fires that summer.

Wrote one Smoke Jumper:

Each [fire] offered special problems both in jumping and in fire-fighting. At the Lembi fire the boys had to dodge rattlesnakes. On Granite Ridge there wasn't any dirt. Schumacher and Hulert found one ideal jumper fire: right at the edge of a meadow, forty yards from a spring, only a quarter-acre in area, with plenty of mineral soil—the textbook example. But you never know what it will be when you hear "Fire on the Mountain!"

The prevention and fighting of forest fires occupied nearly one-fourth of all CPS man-days. CPS operated 31 Forest Service camps. During New Deal days the Civilian Conservation Corps had provided manpower for many Forest Service projects. In 1942 the CCC was disbanded. CPS took up the work.

Most men worked out of base camps, usually several hundred

*CPS men at Camp Royalston carry special pump equipment to a fire in Massachusetts (CPS #10).*

men per camp. In the West the men were often dispersed to remote "spike camps" deep in the mountains. Food and mail arrived once a week. The only breaks in the monotony were the grueling battles with forest fires. Most of the work was fire prevention, building trails and fire roads, opening firebreaks and clearing out underbrush and rotting timber. It was hard physical labor. More technical tasks were telephone line building and maintenance, and manning fire lookout towers.

Forestry work also involved timber-stand improvement. At Medaryville, Indiana, CPS men raised millions of seedlings and planted them in burned over areas. Near Waldport, Oregon, a million seedlings were planted on one 1,600 acre "burn." Woodland improvement involved timber surveying, estimating yields and marking trees for cutting.

Some of the most interesting forestry work was in the San Dimas National Forest in California, where CPS men worked on a 50-year analysis of the main watershed for Los Angeles County. They checked rain gauges, recorded water runoff and tabulated and analyzed the results. Out of the work came a detailed life history of a drop of water as it fell on the rocks and forests of the area. This became the basis for new water management and water retention techniques.

At CPS #12 near Cooperstown, New York, a CPS man invented a gadget which quickly calculated the yield of a stand of timber, saving time for foresters doing timber surveys. Another CPSer, a sociologist, used opinion testing techniques to develop a new public education program for the Forest Service.

One of the most interesting Forest Service camps was CPS #31 near Camino, California. A large Mennonite-administered camp, nearly half of the men were non-Mennonite. The camp was near fruit orchards and the men were sometimes asked to do emergency farm work for the orchardists. The pay for the work went into the Federal Treasury. Some of the men objected to this, arguing that the money would in effect be supporting the war effort. Others believed the work contributed to food production and offered an opportunity to witness for peace to the community. Since Selective Service insisted the money be placed in the Federal Treasury, NSBRO terminated work for the orchardists.

The men at Camino highlighted another problem. The work supervisors at Camino remembered the CCC days at the camp and geared the work to that level of performance. The result was a lot of dissatisfaction with the work schedules. The camp paper, *The Snow-liner,* reported:

Production schedules are still based on CCC and WPA

**Comment by someone visiting Sideling Hill CPS camp:**
*He said ". . . he never saw such a godforsaken place in his life. He felt surely that he had come into a concentration camp."*

records while it is a proven fact that CPS men work more rapidly. Some of the forestry men have the idea we have been sent here as punishment rather than as an alternative to military service. Another camper described his frustrations:

Our crew leaves at any time between 7:30 and 8:00 a.m. It seems to make little difference. Then we drive until about 9:30 and arrive at the proposed place of work. After another 30 minutes of doing practically nothing, finally by 10 we begin on

*These men are doing a forest survey, a major task under the Forest Service. This crew is at Cooperstown, New York (CPS #12, AFSC).*

the job. At 11:45 we stop for dinner, at 1:15 we begin work, at 3:30 we get into the truck and start for camp. We arrive there any time between 4:30 and 4:45 p.m. and call it a day. It hurts my conscience to put time in that way when at home we were used to doing an honest day's work and now they need my services there so badly.

It must be pointed out that while Camino seemed overstaffed to some of its men, their purpose for being there was to fight fires. Supervisors came up with make-work to keep everyone employed between fires.

## National Park Service

Work for the National Park Service involved far fewer men than the Forest Service. All but two of the eight camps were located in the

*Hard physical labor was the lot of many CPS men. These men are from CPS #23, Coshocton, Ohio.*

East; in the West the Mennonites operated camps at Three Rivers, California, and at Belton, Montana. The National Parks assignments were fire-fighting and park maintenance. The latter was usually unpopular; "manicuring the trees" as the CPSers derisively called it. On the Blue Ridge Parkway and the Skyline Drive in Virginia CPS men did "vista-schnitten," cutting trees and underbrush to open up views over the Shenandoah Valley. Many of the campgrounds and roadways in the parks today are a product of CPS labor.

Camp #45 near Luray, Virginia, was established in August 1942 and soon had 150 men assigned to it. Its location near the center of the Shenandoah National Park facilitated access to work projects north and south in the Park. The men engaged in a variety of jobs, some interesting and some tedious. One of the least popular, but important, was blister rust control. This involved pulling out gooseberry bushes, and when their roots broke off, pouring salt into the hole. About the only excitement was meeting rattlesnakes at close range. The crew claimed they collected a rattler nearly every day.

Much of the men's energy went into construction projects. They built a fire lookout tower and a cabin on the summit of Hogback Mountain, elevation 3,474 feet, during the winter of 1942–43. Much of the time the fog was so thick the men could not see the bottom of the 35-foot tower from the top. When they built the Old Rag Mountain tower in 1943 they had to hand-carry all the material more than a mile up a 45-degree grade to the building site.

The most exciting work was fire fighting. All of the men were members of fire-fighting crews, usually in groups of 20–25 men. In the four years of the camp they fought many fires, although there were fewer fires than in the West.

Morale at Luray was generally good, but in 1944 when volunteers were solicited to open a new camp at Belton, Montana, many key men at Luray volunteered for the transfer, only to learn that the Park Service supervisors refused to release them. The result was hard feelings on both sides. The strain required a lot of effort to mend relationships between the CPSers and their supervisors.

## Soil Conservation

One out of every six man-days worked by CPSers was in soil conservation activity. Twenty-three camps worked in Soil Conservation Service projects, with a few devoted to Farm Security Administration and Bureau of Reclamation projects. Because of the size of their projects, these camps were among the largest in CPS.

The men constructed 49 sizable dams, 164 reservoirs and 200 smaller dams. They built many miles of fence, sodded a million and a half square yards of gullies and slopes, dug 680,000 feet of ditches and 2,870 miles of contour furrows, moved 16 million yards of dirt and muck while cleaning canals and levees, and built 2,670 water control structures for irrigation.

Nearly all CPSers spent time at this hard, menial and tedious work. Digging postholes, grubbing weeds and shoveling gravel and muck seldom seemed to meet the definition of "work of national importance." Many men escaped as soon as they could arrange a transfer to another task.

But there was important work to be done. In Washington County, Maryland, the soil conservation agent, Wilbur H. Stevenson, needed help to improve local soil conservation practices. Since

*A fire lookout tower near North Fork, California (CPS #35, MCC).*

there was no CCC camp in the area, he proposed the creation of a number of small units of CPS men who would live on farms, be close to their work projects, and experiment with small-scale subsistence agriculture which might be instructive for demobilized soldiers who wanted to be farmers when the War ended. CPS like the idea as an experiment in small-unit administration and an opportunity to have the men produce much of their own food.

The Mennonites bought three farms and the Brethren bought two. All five small units were administered as CPS #24, but each farmstead operated its program independently. Usually two or three men operated the farm and the rest of the men worked on soil conservation projects in Washington County. After hours, they too helped on the farm, fixing farm buildings, gardening and caring for the livestock.

Unit Three was owned and operated by the Amish, who paid for all maintenance expenses. Nearly all the assignees were Amish.

*Men lining an irrigation ditch with rocks near Colorado Springs, Colorado (CPS #5, MCC).*

*CPS men doing research in soil erosion in the chemical laboratory at CPS #23, Coshocton, Ohio.*

Reflecting their close community ties, the members of this small unit had the distinction of having more visitors from home in one year than any other CPS camp.

One of the most sophisticated projects was at Coshocton, Ohio, where CPS men staffed a Soil Conservation Service experiment station. They researched the relationships between soil type, humidity and plants. Soil samples from all over the state of Ohio were analyzed by the men. One CPSer, a professional botanist, made a comprehensive study of the plant life of Ohio. CPS mathematicians produced statistical analyses for the project. Others designed technical equipment for use in experiments.

Some projects had almost immediate effect on the life and well-being of the people in the area. For centuries the Pocomoke River on the eastern shore of Maryland had flooded the flatlands and made the rich soil useless for agriculture. If its riverbed were

*Ed Maldaner (left) said of this photo: "I didn't just pose for the picture. I was busy giving testimony." Ed and his co-worker were on the project at CPS #94 (AFSC) near Trenton, North Dakota.*

straightened and cleaned out, the Pocomoke would flow swiftly into the Chesapeake Bay and not flood the farmland on its banks. CPS took on the project. Using raw muscle, linked with bulldozers and draglines, the muck-choked channel of the river was cleaned. Only months later lush fields of corn and vegetables grew where before there had been only swamp.

CPS undertook farm reclamation and development on a large scale in North Dakota and Montana. There thousands of farms were destroyed during the drought of 1935–37. CPS Camp Terry near

Terry, Montana, on the banks of the Yellowstone River was established in January 1943. Working for the Farm Security Administration, CPS men built irrigation dams, canals and ditches, leveled the land with bulldozers, and built new farmsteads. On each 80- or 160-acre unit they built a house, barn and poultry house. Through local cooperatives these new farms were allocated to farmers who had lost their land during the drought of the 1930s.

At Hill City, North Dakota, CPS built Deerfield Dam, designed to supply water to Rapid City and irrigate 12,000 acres of farmland in the area. Water made the production of sugar beets possible. The dam was huge—137 feet high and 800 feet long.

The men operated heavy earth-moving equipment and poured vast amounts of concrete for the sluiceways and conduits. The weather and the environment were harsh; work in the winter time continued even when temperatures plummeted to 48 degrees below zero. Since the location of the camp was on a high plateau, even in summer there was occasional frost. The men suffered much sickness, including serious cases of influenza and stomach ulcers. The

*A CPS-operated Soil Conservation Service dragline at work in Caroline County, Maryland (CPS #52, AFSC-MCC).*

bleak isolation of the camp was also a problem; it was 40 miles to the nearest town.

*Orin "Robbie" Robinson, clearing crew foreman at Powellsville, Maryland (CPS #52, MCC).*

## Food Production

The war created vast food shortages. Many CPS men were farmers and longed to use their skills for what they considered a critical need. Farmers, short of labor as millions of young men were drafted, pled for help from the COs. The Historic Peace Churches wanted to boost food production to help supply war-devastated parts of the world.

Selective Service feared adverse public reaction to replacing drafted farmhands with COs. The Comptroller General ruled that all wages earned by COs would have to be turned over to the United States Treasury. The COs faced a conscience problem since the money would be used to finance the war. But the farm crisis became so acute that by the spring of 1943 a plan was developed to place 500 men on dairy farms.

The War Food Administration identified 27 counties which suffered serious shortages of dairy-farm labor. County agents assigned the men to farms and contracted the terms of employment. To satisfy HPC concerns, wages were paid not to the COs, but to NSBRO. After the expenses of the program were deducted the balance was turned over to the Treasury, where the money was placed in a special account to be held until the end of the war.

*CPS men designed and built this posthole digger which could dig two miles of postholes in a day (CPS #33, Fort Collins, Colorado, MCC).*

Nearly 200 men became milk testers. Their task was to keep production records for farmers who were members of cooperative cow-testing associations. On a monthly rotation the tester traveled to one farm each day where he recorded the milk production of each cow in the herd. The point of the work was to use the records to weed out poor producers and to link feeding schedules to each cow's milk production. The benefits were substantial increases in milk production and efficiency.

Some men in the dairy program also worked with artificial breeding associations as technicians and inseminators. The hope was that the experience would be useful after the War when relief agencies would try to rebuild dairy herds destroyed by the War.

CPS men worked at agricultural schools and experimental farms. At Beltsville, Maryland, a unit of 25 men managed the experimental herd of 500 dairy cows. In Nebraska CPS men did experiments on grasses and seeds. At Ames, Iowa, 50 Friends CPSers operated a crop-breeding program, cultivating small plots of different strains, testing and comparing the results with other plots.

All of these projects made possible the continuation of long-range experiments designed to improve the quality and yield of crops and animals. The COs hoped their work would increase the amount of food available to a starving, war-shattered world.

No aspect of the CPS farm program created greater controversy than the Selective Service decision to use CPS men for emergency farm labor in areas within a 15 mile radius of a CPS camp. Whenever a county agent in such an area decided conditions required it, he could authorize their labor. The HPCs and the men were very upset by this order. Not only did such work supersede the camp project work, but it took no account of the wishes of the men. Wages were transferred to the U.S. Treasury. In all, 150,000 man-hours of emergency farm work was performed by CPS. Most men participated reluctantly; some refused to cooperate. The activity came very close to a showdown between CPS on one side and Selective Service and the farmers on the other.

# 5

# Mentalᅠ
# Health

*Byberry buildings at the Philadelphia State Hospital (CPS #49, AFSC).*

When 22-year-old Henry Claassen left Beatrice, Nebraska, in July 1942 he became a member of recently opened CPS #33 near Fort Collins, Colorado. CPS #33 was a Soil Conservation Service project. Claassen found the work "contrived and boring," so boring that he put on weight. When he heard that they were recruiting volunteers to establish a CPS unit at Ypsilanti State Hospital in Michigan, he jumped at the chance for a change and became one of the founders of the new mental hospital unit. He found his work as an attendant immensely satisfying. It seemed to square with his pacifist convictions, with his reasons for being in CPS.

Claassen's dissatisfaction with base camp work was widely

shared. By 1942 CPSers were developing a ground swell of interest in working in social welfare. Selective Service resisted the idea, fearing adverse public opinion. An obtuse argument was that COs should not be placed in institutions where they could spread their philosophy or harm the war effort.

The need for mental hospital attendants was overwhelming. The staffs of mental hospitals were decimated by the onset of the War as hospital employees moved on to better paying jobs in the new war economy. Mental hospital staffs were notoriously ill paid.

In 1941 Philadelphia State Hospital had 1,000 employees. By October 1942 only 200 remained. Designed for 2,500 patients, the hospital held 6,000. There was one attendant for 300 patients. They had a desperate need for more attendants.

In June 1942 the first CPS unit began work at Eastern State Hospital in Williamsburg, Virginia, and in July a second unit opened at Western State Hospital in Staunton, Virginia. Once begun the mental hospital units grew rapidly. Eventually there were CPS men in 41 mental hospitals in 20 states. More than 2,000 men worked in the program at its height.

Most CPS men worked as ward attendants. Some tended the dairy and vegetable gardens, stoked furnaces and worked in the kitchens. A few assisted in recreational and occupational therapy. The work was hard and long; most men logged at least 72 hours per week and sometimes as much as 100 hours.

At most hospitals the main function of the CPS attendant was to assure custody of the patients. At Eastern State Hospital one attendant was responsible for 100 to 175 patients on the violent ward — a nearly impossible task to manage successfully. A distasteful but necessary assignment was the care of bed patients. Many were incontinent as well as diseased. Changing beds, dressing pressure sores and giving special feedings demanded great patience from the CPSers.

Sometimes CPS men made dramatic changes in the care of patients. At Philadelphia State Hospital patient care was terrible. Because of labor shortages there was one attendant for every 300 patients (minimum set by the Psychiatric Association was 10). Soon after their arrival, 10 of the men volunteered to take over the worst ward in the hospital — the ward for incontinent patients where 350 people lived with almost no care, naked, filthy and ill-fed. The men cleaned and painted the entire building. They installed a new feeding program, encouraging patients to eat slowly instead of bolting down all food in sight. They established a routine morning dressing procedure for all patients. They removed wet fouled clothing immediately. They instituted new schedules to bring some order to pa-

*A CPS attendant at a mental hospital asked a patient who was stumbling unsteadily about the ward if he was drunk. "No," was the quick retort, "just practising."*

tients' lives. The building began to smell better. The improvement was dramatic, largely a result of patience inspired by good will.

In most cases, however, the changes were less dramatic. CPS man J. Willard Linscheid at Hudson River State Hospital reported:

Ward 41 is the largest of the wards with a patient census varying from 110 to 120. The building itself is not fireproof but of brick and frame construction. There are no outside porches for any of the wards.

The patients are all destructive, incontinent, feeble or occasionally assaultive. A number are blind and crippled. There are no working patients capable of taking more than a very negligible amount of responsibility.

When we were put on the ward there was one male registered nurse in charge, two male attendants, one clothes room woman and a woman to take care of the dining room. The daily routine began with getting patients out of bed at 6:00 a.m. and serving breakfast at 7:00 a.m.

An attempt was made to keep about 30 of the most destructive and incontinent patients in one of the small day rooms. Because of the lack of good worker patients and attendant help,

*A CPS man reads to blind mentally ill patients at Byberry Philadelphia State Hospital (CPS #49, AFSC).*

it was impossible for one attendant to keep the room clean, so most times feces and urine puddles were in evidence.

Meals were served in three shifts. First those who were capable of carrying their own trays from the counter came in. Then three tables were set for the assaultive and destructive patients who had to be watched closely and even then would steal food and upset trays. The last group fed were the blind, crippled and feeble. When we arrived the system had been to serve the blind and feeble first. This was usually accomplished in 10 minutes or less. The attendant would wait until about half of the group was out and then begin jerking the trays away from the others to hurry them out. If a patient protested he was forced roughly from the room. Little attempt was made to check if all the patients had been served and often some were deliberately not called either for punishment or because they were "too much trouble to feed."

Because of the large number of incontinent and destructive

*The Dayroom at Philadelphia State Hospital (CPS #49, AFSC).*

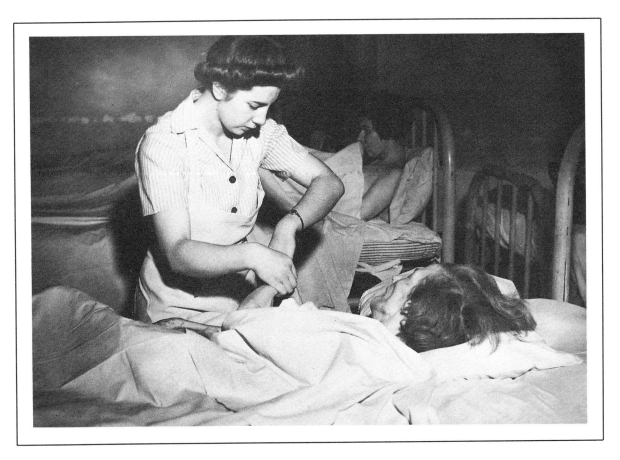

*Ruth Louise Miller checks the pulse of a patient at Cleveland State Hospital. Ruth was a COG, a Conscientious Objector Girl, who may have been a volunteer or an employee of the hospital (CPS #69, AFSC-MCC).*

patients, much clothing was destroyed and soiled so that much of the time the disturbed patients in the small day room were entirely naked. At night the patients were put to bed with their clothes on, and so much was ruined before morning. Because of the wartime shortages of sheets and blankets the majority of patients had only one sheet or one blanket on their beds most of the time. If possible, the disturbed and incontinent patients were also given a blanket or sheet, but much of the time they slept naked and uncovered on the hard canvas mattresses.

We attempted to right some of the many wrongs. Our first move was to shower the soiled patients when necessary. This only increased the lack of clothing and they were naked as often as before. To partially remedy this, two men were put on a 10:00 a.m. to 7:00 p.m. shift. It was their job to undress all the patients, tie and label the clothing of the cleaner ones and sort the clothing of the incontinents. This helped somewhat at keeping at least the cleaner patients clothed.

In the cafeteria we changed the order of groups so that the

feeble and blind were served last and no patient was forced to leave the dining hall before he completed his meal. We also saw to it that every patient was served three meals.

We tried to take the incontinent patients in the disturbed section to the toilet at frequent intervals, although when only one or two men were on duty this was often neglected because of the press of other duties.

Our efforts were concentrated on giving better and kinder

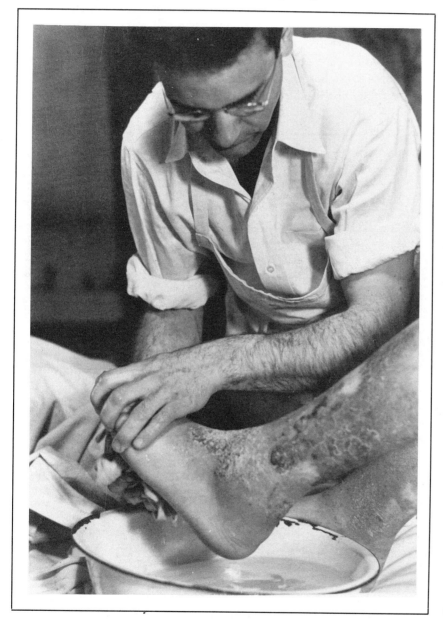

*A CPS man bathes the foot of a mental patient.*

treatment to the patients and to keep the ward as clean as possible under the circumstances. The shortage of floor wax and clothing made it well nigh impossible to do more than keep the ward clean of the worst dirt.

Working a ward such as this one with negligible patient help, almost no supplies, and very poor facilities in general is quite a strain on an attendant. Especially when there are only two or three on duty alone part of the day. When it is impossible to do more than clean the most obvious dirt and possible only to keep the patients as well in order as possible, a sort of lethargy sets in.

I'm sure we all chafed under this necessity of giving only custodial care and we were all keenly aware of the improvements that could be made with more attendant help, more supplies and better facilities. Proper personal attention to any single patient or a small group of patients was out of the ques-

*A CPS man helps a patient "light up" (CPS #63, Marlboro, New Jersey, MCC).*

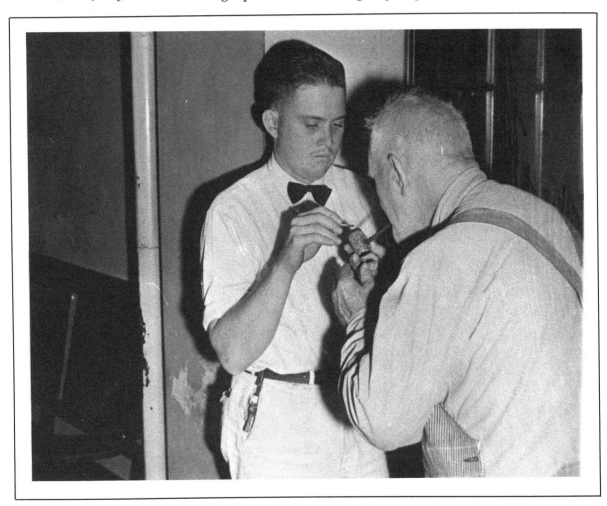

tion.

Consciousness of the large number of patients entrusted to one's care led to a very impersonal attitude toward all of them. Although we were told repeatedly that our handling of patients was much better than that of the former attendants, the frustrations encountered gave rise to fits of temper which at time resulted in unnecessarily rough language and rough handling of patients. This loss of control grew more frequent as the time on the ward grew longer.

The red tape and extremely impersonal institutional attitude

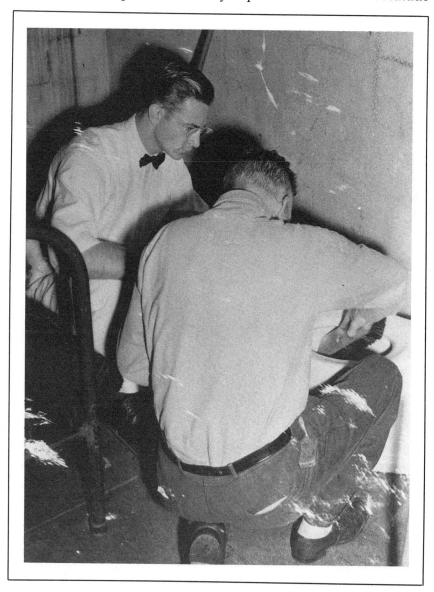

*CPS man Henry Claassen and a colleague do some dirty work at New Jersey State Hospital (CPS #63, MCC).*

involved in getting any consideration from the doctor and higher officials in the service, whose hands were in turn tied by their superiors, developed a feeling of resignation to conditions as they were. Custodial care only was given.

I feel that our most important contribution was in giving more individual care to all the patients and treating them all in a more gentle and humane manner. Formerly a patient who caused trouble at intervals was labeled "bad" and placed in a camisole whenever one was available. We tried to resort to the camisole only when necessary. Sores and unusual symptoms of illness were perhaps noticed more carefully and reported to the charge nurse or doctor. Medications were administered conscientiously resulting in a reduction in the number of epileptic seizures experienced by at least two patients.

I believe we all feel that in improving the physical appearance of the ward we failed almost completely, but in patient care and treatment we improved conditions. This contact with abnormal individuals gave us all a deeper understanding of society

*CPS men help prepare a patient for a shock treatment at Durham, North Carolina (CPS #61, MCWP).*

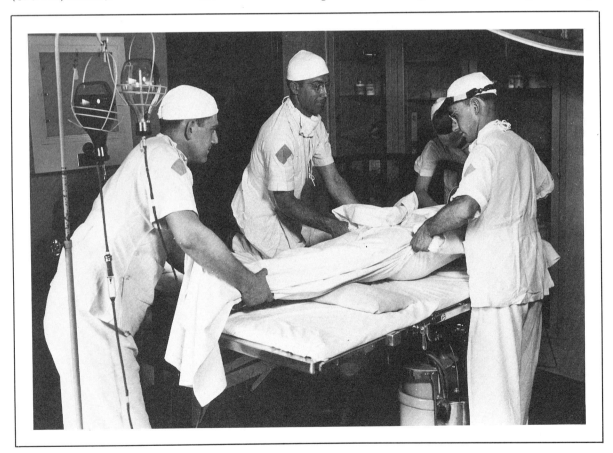

in general and of the evil rampant in the world today.

Our relationships with patients' relatives gave rise to feelings of sympathy and again to feelings of anger and helplessness when we realized our own inability to explain behavior causes and to accomplish any evident improvement in these patients.

I think we were all fired with a desire to expose mental hospital conditions to the general public in the hope that such an exposé would lead to action toward the improvement of such institutions. Certainly to work for any length of time on such a ward a person must either agitate for betterment or sear his conscience entirely to the ills of humanity.

A far better situation met CPSers at Ypsilanti, Michigan. There a relatively new facility with a progressive superintendent offered a much healthier environment in which to work. What the men brought to such a setting was human kindness and care. Furthermore, they helped keep the manpower from dropping to the levels of many other hospitals.

A few CPS men were able to do experimental and remedial work with the mentally ill. A unit at Duke University Hospital worked full-time in the psychiatric ward and, under doctors' direction, administered the most advanced methods of therapy. At the Asheville, North Carolina, hospital they assisted with new deep-shock

*CPS men at Ypsilanti State Hospital discuss the topic "The Church and Mental Hospitals." Discussants are Lotus Troyer, Victor Janzen, Gordon Kaufman, Elmer Buhler, Lloyd Goering, Hubert Moore and Karl Schultz.*

insulin treatments. The results were sometimes striking. "No thrill is comparable to the restoration of a disintegrating personality to a good level of behavior," a CPS man observed.

Patients frequently expressed their gratitude for the work of the CPSers. A patient at Ypsilanti wrote the following poem:

### A Change Has Taken Place

A big change has taken place
    In the hospital here
That has taken away
    All worry and fear.

They have got some new help
    They're a fine bunch of men
And there's surely a difference
    Between now and then.

They call them C.O.s
    And a fine Christian bunch
Who believe in kindness
    With no kick or a punch . . .

So we can all be thankful
    they sent the C.O.s
For it's more like home
    As everyone knows.

Several CPS units worked at training schools for the mentally ill such as the Vineland Institute in Vineland, New Jersey. There the men taught classes and acted as headmasters of cottages. The goal was to teach skills and vocations so that patients might eventually enter self-sustaining occupations.

## Dilemmas Developed

How should COs behave in a situation where use of force and physical violence were often in evidence? This was a major concern of the men. Fortunately both law and the psychiatric profession required nonviolence in handling the patients. In practice a great deal of force came into play. How to handle a ward in turmoil when a patient got out of hand was always a problem. In some wards there was real physical danger to the attendant, as happened at the Byberry Hospital where Bob, a CPS man, was felled one night by a hard right to his jaw as he was trying to put a violent patient to bed. After shaking off his dizziness, Bob picked himself off the floor and continued putting the man to bed as if nothing had happened.

Frank Olmstead, chairman of the War Resisters' League, observed CPS men at work in such situations. He reported:

One objector assigned to a violent ward refused to take the broomstick offered by the Charge. When he entered the ward the patients crowded around asking, "Where is your broomstick?" He said he thought he would not need it. "But suppose some of us gang up on you?" The CO guessed they wouldn't do that and started talking about other things. Within a few days the

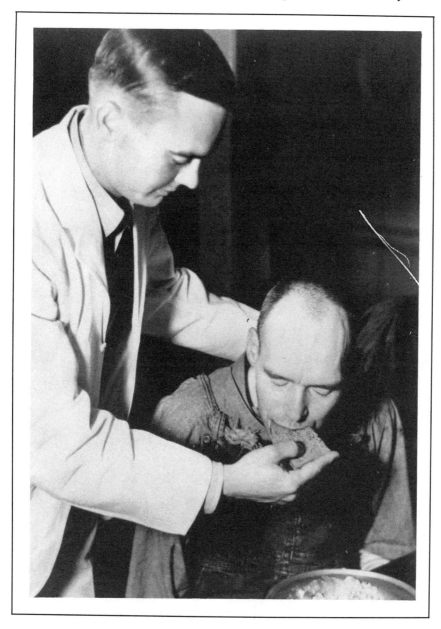

*CPS man feeds a patient at Philadelphia State Hospital (CPS #49, AFSC).*

patients were seen gathering around the unarmed attendant, telling him of their troubles. He felt much safer than the Charge who had only his broomstick for company.

The success of the COs as mental health attendants, Olmstead believed, grew out of their effort to put nonviolence into practice. They were just as fearful of patient violence as the other attendants, but were not so prone to use violence, partly because they wanted to show there was an alternative approach to the problems.

*Unlocking a ward door at Cleveland State Hospital (CPS #69).*

It would be wrong to say that all objectors performed admirably under trying situations. In fact, several were removed from their assignments for excessive violence, and at least one was implicated as an accomplice in the death of an unruly patient. Most came to terms with the need to use restraining force, particularly when patients threatened harm to others or to themselves.

The reforms and new emphases of the CPS men were not always kindly received by their fellow workers. At the Hudson River State

*At the Staunton, Virginia hospital, a patient asked if a certain clock showed the right time. When told it did, he replied, "Well, what is it doing here then?"*

Hospital, several of the men reported violence and physical abuse on the part of regular employees. As a result, four employees were immediately dismissed. Two were war veterans, and three were members of the American Federation of Labor. Soon front page stories and editorials appeared in the Poughkeepsie newspapers. The American Legion demanded that the dismissed men be given hearings and accused the director of the hospital of coddling the CPSers. The storm soon passed when it became clear that the director and the CPS men had acted completely within the requirements of the law.

For many CPS men their mental hospital experience made a lasting impression on their lives. Wrote one:

> I would consider the hospital work by far the most significant of any I did while in CPS. There is something about seeing a demented person return to normalcy which raises a lump in your throat; you grope for words to express it. I had that experience several times.

One of the important outcomes of the mental hospital CPS work was a movement called the Mental Health Hygiene Program which later became the National Mental Health Foundation. The impetus for this came out of the Friends unit at Byberry Hospital in Philadelphia. Four men in the unit — Willard Hetzel, Leonard Edelstein, Phil Steer and Harold Barton — wanted to find a way to communicate their ideas and develop long-range reform programs. Out of their interest came *The Attendant* magazine, edited by Phil Steer. The group also proposed an ambitious survey of conditions in mental hospitals. To get the work done the men were given detached service status.

In May 1946 the Mental Hygiene Project became the National Mental Health Foundation, and *The Attendant* became a professional journal, *The Psychiatric Aide*. The mental hospital survey became a book, **Out of Sight — Out of Mind,** written by Frank L. Wright, Jr., a CPS man who had worked at the Greystone Park CPS unit in New Jersey.

Out of their wartime experience, the Mennonites and others developed a number of mental health facilities. Of all the CPS projects the mental health program seems most integral to the convictions and purpose of CPS.

# 6

# Social Work

Several CPS programs tried to remedy social ills and improve the health of ordinary people. In five Florida counties where hookworm infected up to 80% of the population, CPS men were employed by the Florida State Public Health Board to fight the parasites. The solution was to build sanitary privies to halt the spread of the larvae.

In March 1942 the Brethren opened CPS #27 near Tallahassee. Within a few months the Mennonites and Friends added other units at Mulberry, Orlando and Gainesville.

The men developed a masterful system to construct privies and install them. Their best construction time was 2.86 man-days as

*These privies are being loaded for transport to the installation sites as part of the hookworm project in Florida (CPS #27, BSC).*

against the earlier New Deal WPA record of 11.75 man-days per structure. By the time the men left they had built and installed 4,200 privies, dug countless wells and installed hundreds of septic tanks. It was a program which assisted the poorest of the poor, mostly black Floridians.

The men also worked at other public health problems. One man toured the state in a "dentmobile" as a dental assistant, caring for the teeth of school children too poor to get ordinary treatment. A

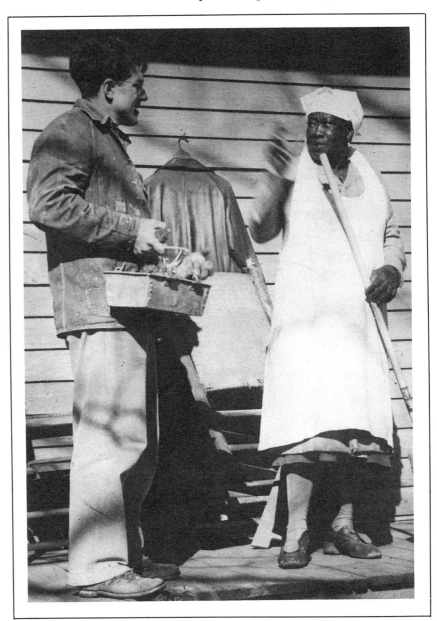

*Making a contact on the typhus control program (CPS #141, Gulfport, Mississippi, MCC).*

thorough sanitary survey of Polk County was made in the process of "selling" the installation of the privies. Even Selective Service was impressed. "The hookworm project will stand out as one of the most worthwhile contributions made by the C.O.s in this war," an SS officer declared after visiting the project.

Early in the history of CPS, its leaders became aware of needs in Puerto Rico. In June 1942 the Martin G. Brumbaugh Reconstruction unit began work on the island. Puerto Rico was overpopulated, undernourished, with massive heath problems. Hookworm, tuberculosis, malaria, syphilis and intestinal diseases raged at near epidemic levels. There was one doctor for every 5,000 people, with little or no health care available in the countryside. The War aggravated all of these problems. The Puerto Rican Reconstruction Administration (PRRA), created in 1935 as part of the New Deal, had been working at rural development, but since the War began had lost nearly all of its funding.

With PRRA blessing, the Brethren built and staffed a 26 bed hospital in the village of Castaner. With two outlying dispensaries the hospital was able to serve the health needs of 20,000 people in a thirty-mile radius. Aggressive immunization programs were initiated for smallpox, typhoid fever and diphtheria. The Mennonites established a similar hospital at La Plata and the Friends opened a clinic at Zalduondo.

The CPS units worked at malnutrition, establishing milk stations where youngsters were served breakfast. The government provided the milk and CPS the manpower. CPSers also promoted gardening. They placed a special emphasis on growing soybeans to raise the protein level of diets. Some of these measures were carried out through newly created 4-H clubs.

Among the most challenging assignments for CPS men were the guinea pig experiments under the Office of Scientific Research or under the Surgeon General's Office. Though the projects were often uncomfortable and dangerous, there were always plenty of volunteers. In New England several researchers at Harvard Medical School used CPS men to search for a cheap control for the dreaded disease typhus. The men wore lice-infested clothes for three weeks while continuing to work at their daily nine hours of road-building. Each day they were inspected and dusted with powders designed to kill the lice. Eventually two safe and effective powders were found.

Infectious hepatitis was one of the wartime epidemic diseases for which no one could determine its cause, how it spread or how to treat it effectively. Experiments were done on CPS men at mental hospitals and, later, units of 30 to 60 men at the University of Pennsylvania and at Yale University engaged in full-scale projects.

*The story goes that a Chicago "boy" filled out his form 47 to reflect his opposition to war in any form. The local board refused to consider his request for CO status, and classified him I-A. The Appeal Board, however, gave him his sought after IV-E, whereupon the draft board immediately classified him IV-F, justifying the change with the notation, "inability to reason."*

The men were inoculated with blood plasma suspected of being infectious, swallowed nose and throat washings and body wastes of infected patients, and drank contaminated water. It was found that an elusive virus is apparently responsible for hepatitis, and that the disease can be transmitted not only through human filth but via serum and drinking water.

More than 100 CPSers scientifically caught the common cold by inhaling or drinking throat washings taken from soldiers with colds and pneumonia. The tests, conducted at CPS camp Rufus Jones at Gatlinburg, Tennessee, and at Holly Inn, Pinehurst, North Carolina, proved that colds and pneumonia are caused by a virus and not by bacteria.

The war in the Pacific made malaria a deadly threat for American troops. Its cause was well-known — mosquitoes carried the bacteria from an infected person. The problem was the cure: the most effective was heavy doses of quinine, but it was virtually unobtainable since its souces lay behind Japanese lines. New drugs had been developed to replace quinine but had never been tried on human subjects. CPS men agreed to try.

*Weighing food for men acting as guinea pigs in the CPS protein and vitamin experiment. The experiments were directed by the Harvard Fatigue Laboratory, sponsored by the National Research Council (CPS #32, West Campton, New Hampshire, AFSC).*

*A CPS social worker talks with one of the youngsters at the Cheltenham, Maryland School for Boys, a facility for juvenile offenders. The CPS staff was interracial (CPS #62, AFSC).*

The tests were conducted at the University of Chicago Medical School, Columbia, Stanford and Cornell universities, and at Massachusetts General Hospital. The most dangerous tests were those in which the men allowed themselves to be bitten by bacteria-carrying mosquitoes. When their fever reached its height, after three or four days, they were given the new medicines. Some of the drugs eventually proved superior to quinine as a treatment for malaria.

At the University of Minnesota 12 CPS volunteers tested the physiological effects of malaria. Each man contracted malaria and went through the various stages of the illness. The illness was then terminated with quinine sulphate. After their temperatures returned to normal, the men resumed their usual work, but each day exercised on a treadmill for an hour. Over the course of two months, tests were performed which indicated the debilitating effects of the illness and the time necessary for full recovery.

The War on the oceans lent urgency to learning more about survival in the event of a ship sinking. What were the effects of drinking salt water? What kind of rations should be stocked in lifeboats? Several CPS men drank salt water. Others ate the official navy rations stocked in life rafts. Several in the latter experiment ended up in the emergency ward of the hospital. It was determined that a simple ration of candy and water was best for lifeboat diets.

*A light-hearted view by a CPS man of the experiment to see if one could survive by eating pelleted grass.*

A major threat to surviving in a life raft is the evaporation of body liquid. Five CPSers spent two weeks in a life raft in Cotuit Bay near Boston. They discovered that they could eliminate almost entirely the loss of body water by soaking their clothes and hanging over the side of the raft for five minutes every half hour.

Nearly 300 guinea pigs tested various nutrition problems. At the University of Illinois Research Hospital they sat for hours at temperatures 20 degrees below zero to see the effect of extreme cold on controlled diets. Others did the same thing in "ovens." Others sat in pressure chambers simulating high altitudes for the same reason. At a New Hampshire CPS camp the Harvard Fatigue Laboratory put men on restricted diets on the "Iron Maiden," a wooden step 16 inches high. Carrying a 65-pound pack, the volunteers stepped up and down on the step every two seconds for five minutes or until they passed out.

At CPS Camp Magnolia in Arkansas, 50 volunteers ate dehydrated grass tips for three months to see if that might be a relief substitute for fruits and vegetables. It was not.

Dr. Ancel Keys at the University of Minnesota Laboratory of Physiological Hygiene designed what was probably the most dramatic of these nutrition experiments. The purpose was to find the most effective food relief for war-devastated areas with inadequate food resources. Thirty-six CPS men volunteered to go through a three-month period on a normal diet of 3,200 calories, followed by a six-month period on 1,800 calories. This was less than the amount of food most commonly available under European famine conditions. A rehabilitative period completed the experiment.

The results were significant. The ability to sustain physical work fell drastically, as did sustained intellectual effort. The education program in which the men were engaged simply collapsed. Craving for food became their single preoccupation; nothing else mattered. Many showed a tendency toward introversion and lethargy. Their recovery was much slower than anyone expected. Most striking was the failure of an upturn in their morale and spirits as the men returned to an adequate diet. In fact, the men experienced a slump in morale, they were irritable and struggled with serious depression. The aftereffects were so severe that most of the men indicated they would not have volunteered had they known how rigorous the experiment would be.

The results of the experiment were made available to all the major relief agencies concerned with postwar food and nutrition problems, including government agencies. The experiment became essential to proper planning and application of postwar relief operations.

# 7

# Life in an Alternative Community

Phil Frey, a Mennonite minister and a regional director of MCC CPS, preaching at a worship service at the Weeping Water, Nebraska camp (CPS #25, MCC).

CPS developed because a faith community was opposed to war. The program offered many by-products, among them the opportunity for CPSers to demonstrate an alternative lifestyle. But the immense diversity of the people participating in CPS, and their traditions, made the goal difficult in practice. The common denominator among the men was their opposition to war. Beyond that, their search for common ground was often hard and unsuccessful.

There was denominational diversity. Over 200 religious groups were involved in CPS, and 400 men claimed no religious identity at all. Mennonites represented 40% of the total; the Church of the Brethren had 11%; the Friends 7%. About 15% came from major

Protestant denominations, with the Methodists having the largest group. The following list offers a general denominational breakdown of the men who served in CPS:

| | |
|---|---:|
| Baptist, Northern | 178 |
| Baptist, Southern | 45 |
| Catholic | 149 |
| Christadelphian | 127 |
| Church of the Brethren | 1,353 |
| Church of Christ | 78 |
| Congregational Christian | 209 |
| Disciples of Christ | 78 |
| Episcopal | 88 |
| Evangelical | 50 |
| Evangelical and Reformed | 101 |
| Friends | 951 |
| German Baptist Brethren | 157 |
| Jehovah's Witnesses | 409 |
| Lutheran | 108 |
| Mennonite | 4,665 |
| Methodist | 673 |
| Presbyterian | 192 |
| Russian Molokan | 76 |
| Unitarians | 44 |
| Other religious groups | 1,695 |
| Unaffiliated | 449 |
| Total | 11,996 |

Mennonite camps nearly always had a majority of Mennonite CPSers. This gave their camps a specific social and religious character.

Mennonites worked hard to keep unity and harmony in their camps. They respected authority and had similar educational and life experiences. As a result, their camps were often placid compared to some of the other CPS camps.

Friends camps were quite diverse. Friends were rarely more than one-third of the assignees in their camps. The Friends' stress on truth as an individual matter promoted a variety of opinion, quite unlike the Mennonites, and made the search for community more difficult.

A collage of peaceful idealists, CPS required a stressful social adjustment for most men. That reality made peace and reconciliation everyday challenges. Not only were they objecting to war, but CPS men were constantly challenged to put their convictions about peace to work in their own camps.

Since CPS was an explicitly religious program one might have expected religious faith to help weld the community together. It is

**CPS had its own lingo:**

*"Briar"—reference to a CPS man*

*"Hoosow"—expression of disgust*

*"Hammerhead", as in "What's the matter with you hammerheads?"*

*"Horsh and gogle"—a lottery technique to dispose of leftover food at the table.*

*"Choke sandwich"—peanut butter sandwich*

*"binder"—cheese sandwich*

*"slider"—jelly sandwich*

*"leathernecks"—pancakes*

*"belt dressing"—syrup*

*"crud"—food*

*"sugar report"—letter from a girl*

*"inmates with keys"—reference to mental hospital attendants*

*Aleem Whitson, a Moslem CPS man, working in the laundry at Merom, Indiana (CPS #14, AFSC).*

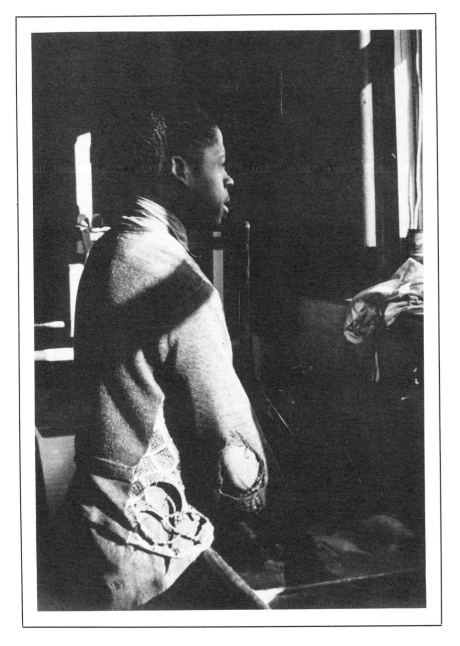

difficult to see that that actually happened. There was something about CPS which made religious activity difficult. Perhaps it was the enforced and sometimes aimless work, the routine and isolation, the service for the "duration," or the dormitory character of life—in any case, spiritual nurture required continual effort.

The Mennonites probably did the best in this regard. The camp director, appointed by the religious agencies, was the "spiritual leader and counselor of the men," and usually had a committee of campers plan and set the pace for religious activities in the camp. Attending religious services was a basic expectation for all Mennonite men. Visiting ministers frequently participated. Good planning, stimulus from the administration and strong home-church influence contributed to the religious life of the Mennonite camps.

The Brethren depended on the initiative of the campers to direct religious activity. Often camps elected religious life secretaries who were given time from project work to plan and lead worship and religious study activities. Toward the end of CPS some of the larger Brethren units had pastors assigned to head the religious program for the men.

The Friends emphasized individual seeking rather than a directed pattern of religious practice. They encouraged daily meetings for meditation and prayer, and Sunday worship as a way to deepen religious experience. Interesting and provocative speakers frequently visited with many positive benefits for the men.

In detached units, such as mental hospitals, the men were able to attend local churches. A great deal of good came from such contacts, both for the men and for the churches involved. Many men sang in

*"Bull session" with Tom Jones, first director of Friends CPS and President of Fiske University. This was a popular way for CPS men to stay abreast of new ideas and developments (CPS #23, Coshocton, Ohio, AFSC).*

*Sunday night hymn sing at Camp Coshocton (CPS #23, AFSC).*

choirs and taught Sunday School, offering the CPSers a connection to the outside world, as well as an opportunity to use their gifts in religiously significant ways.

Virtually all CPS men testified to the benefits of interacting with a variety of religious beliefs. A Brethren CPSer observed, "The men cannot live, work and play together without having a greater appreciation of the other's view." Said a Mennonite, "Mennonites were forced to rethink their own positions and to decide what was mere tradition and custom in their practices and beliefs, as over against what was basic and biblical. Mennonitism, therefore, was subjected to searching analyses so that its weaknesses and its strong points were brought into clear light."

Several interesting religious experiments were undertaken by CPS men on their own initiative. At the Coshocton, Ohio, camp, seven men engaged in a routine of meditation which led to "A Way of Life" commitment—through "active desire, expectant receptivity and resolute action one's life may be advanced toward that greatest of all goals: making the most of one's potentialities as a son of God."

A promising, but unrealized project was begun at Cades Cove, Tennessee, where 12 CPS men gathered to seclude themselves in a permanent retreat for spiritual renewal and practice, while working on a Park Service project. Unfortunately the unit was barely underway before the men were demobilized in 1946.

Moral standards were always a concern in CPS. Smoking, card-playing and drinking were temptations for some. Drinking was strongly discouraged throughout the system. Beards, rough speech, slovenly beds, pin-ups, bizarre lighting and eccentric behavior caused some disturbance, but were usually not serious problems. There were a few serious moral breaches, but on the whole, the moral tone and practice of CPS men were unusually high, given the frustration and boredom which characterized so much of CPS life.

In a survey of Mennonite CPS men in 1946, Paul Albrecht found that 76% of the men believed they had "gained some understanding of the Christian life which the home church needed." This sense of spiritual growth was echoed by other CPSers as well.

*Mealtime at Weeping Water Camp in Nebraska (CPS #25, MCC).*

CPS did not develop a coherent spiritual brotherhood or a corporate spiritual discipline. While religiously based, the CPS consensus opposing the War was not transformed into a spiritual movement. Perhaps it could not be so, given the enormous diversity of history and tradition within the program. CPS spawned spiritual renewal for many; it did not become a unified religious movement.

## Education in CPS

Selective Service regulations were explicit: "An educational program for the men in the camp will be a responsibility of the camp director." The church service agencies endorsed the idea and, in their own way, developed programs.

There were major hurdles to overcome. Education had to be added to the work project. As one observer noted, "The camps were work camps and not schools. When men worked a full day at physical labor out in the wind and the cold air and then sat in a warm classroom, only the most interesting classes could keep many of them awake." CPS leaders hoped to prepare the men for leadership in peacemaking and human service work, but most of the men were

*Doing kitchen chores at Weeping Water Camp, Nebraska (CPS #25, MCC).*

*Peeling potatoes, a never-ending chore (CPS #23, AFSC).*

incurably vocational in their educational goals.

The Mennonites stressed four goals in their educational program: instruction in Mennonite heritage and mission, clarifying Christians' relation to the state and their communities, deepening spiritual experience and promoting personal growth by teaching skills with occupational benefit for the men. The core course was a three-month Mennonite heritage study which all men were strongly urged to take upon arrival. It helped clarify their common purpose which was based on Mennonite theology and history.

Each Mennonite camp had an educational director, and his program was coordinated by an educational secretary at MCC headquarters in Akron. The Brethren had a similar program.

The Brethren program was tailored to the interests of their men. They developed the most effective educational program in CPS by developing the specialized school. Here, men with a common interest were brought together in a camp or unit to focus on a carefully planned course of study. An early and unusual one was located at

*Doing the laundry at Camp Coshocton, Ohio (CPS #23, AFSC).*

Waldport, Oregon, where persons interested in the arts were brought together. Their work, literary and visual, was insightful. There was also a Psychiatry and Christian Service School, an Education Workshop, a School of Industrial Relations, a School of Race Relations, and others. The Mennonites developed a Farm and Community School in connection with their model farm near Hagerstown, Maryland.

Training for relief and reconstruction was popular. At one point 250 men enrolled in a three-month course at several church colleges in preparation for overseas relief appointments, only to have Congress pass legislation forbidding COs to leave the country. But relief-training courses continued to be popular even though there was no immediate prospect for service abroad. A surprising number of CPS men elected a term of relief service after discharge at the end of the War.

Special CPS units located in metropolitan areas offered distinct opportunities for education. A few men earned vocational credentials as part of their work. Eleven men at the Alexian Brothers Hospital in Chicago earned R.N. degrees from the school of nursing while serving as orderlies.

A variety of journalistic activities emerged out of the fertile brains of the CPS men. Almost every camp and unit published a newsletter or bulletin which reported on camp affairs and often on larger issues as well. These materials give insight to the pulse of the various camp settings. Equally interesting are the camp yearbooks, complete with pictures and literary products by the men. Experienced as a gadfly by CPS administrators, *The Pacifica Views*, published at Glendora, California, by Camp #76, intended to pose important issues confronting pacifists.

All camps had libraries, some with sizable collections. Cascade Locks, Oregon (#21), had 3,000 volumes; many camps had as many as 1,500 books. Many camps were able to show films of interest to the men; a number reported viewing the film "Grapes of Wrath." But the greatest learning came from the non-stop bull sessions carried on by the men as they were at work on the project, in the dormitories and in the dining hall. One observer who frequently

*Men in the well-stocked library at the Grottoes, Virginia camp (CPS #4, MCC).*

*While taking a shower one morning, Henry Bowman was heard muttering "Brrr, this hot water sure is cold!"*

visited CPS units was impressed that "stereotypes of all sorts had worn thin. Much vague idealism and romanticism, I felt, had been cut away by the two or three years experience in CPS's hard school."

Thomas Waring reports a discussion which was perennial among CPS men:

"How can you deal with Hitler without violence?"

"That's a tough one. I have no answer either."

"Nobody does it seems. If that's so, then what are we doing here?"

"We have to live with the question, while we continue to work

*A. J. Muste, a frequent visitor to CPS camps, inspects a camp book case on peace and nonviolence.*

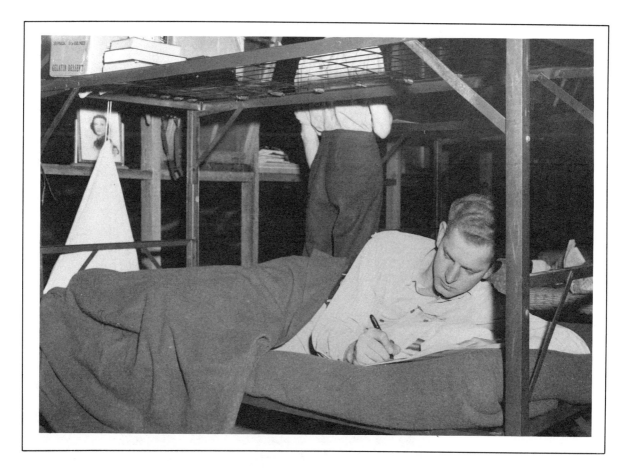

for peace."

"Sure, but our efforts at peacemaking are not stopping Hitler."

"Yes, but stopping Hitler now and preventing future Hitlers are two different things."

Most camps and units had recreation committees to help organize leisure-time activities. Outdoor sports were always popular. Competitive contests pitting barrack against barrack or overhead staff versus project people were common. Most base camps were located in scenic settings with rivers, lakes and mountains nearby, so swimming, hiking and other outdoor physical activities were readily available.

Many camps developed music programs ranging from choirs to informal instrumental ensembles. In some cases, where community relations were good, these efforts were rewarded by invitations to perform in community settings, something much prized by the CPSers.

The most popular activity among campers was crafts. Wood-

*Barrack accommodations. Letter-writing was a major leisure activity (CPS #2, San Dimas, California, AFSC).*

**Sign above a bed in CPS #37, Coleville, CA.**
*"The best nest in the west for a rest."*

*Recreational fads came and went in the camps. Rug making was one of the most persistent (CPS #25, MCC).*

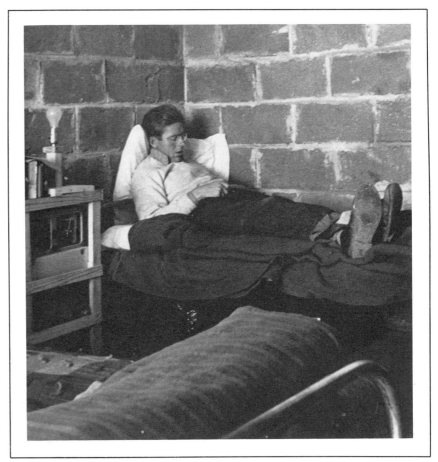

*Rest after a hard day on the project.*

working, rugmaking, leatherwork, photography—all waxed and waned in popularity, but were always in evidence. For a month rugmaking would be a passion with everyone, only to be replaced by a popular enthusiasm for leatherwork. With time on their hands and no money, the men found crafts to be an important way to express their fidelity to their loved ones.

The Brethren camp at Wellston, Michigan (#42), reported, ''Three of the four dorms are now provided with popcorn poppers

**Sign in the Terry, Montana camp dormitory:**
*''Here rest the best snores in the brotherhood.''*

*Letters from home boosted morale (CPS #69, MCC).*

and all have coffee-making equipment. Coffee and popcorn parties are in progress almost every night."

The barracks were usually heated by round cast-iron stoves which glowed with heat and were a natural setting for dormitory gatherings. Often the camaraderie was enhanced by creative fixings from the camp kitchen.

Life in CPS camps was highly informal, a significant difference from military camp routine. This sometimes frustrated military Selective Service people on inspection tours.

Since many men found the $2.50 monthly allowance too slim to cover clothing purchases, many of them wore clothes sent to the camps by church groups. They tended to wear clothes out, so a crew of CPS men on project often had a rather ragged appearance. Socks were especially prone to wear, so a common sight at camp meetings was men industriously darning socks. Much envied were the men whose mothers, wives or girlfriends did the darning chores.

A great morale booster was visits by family, friends and pastors.

*Horseshoes was a popular recreational activity (CPS #6, Lagro, Indiana, BSC).*

They brought relief from the tedium of camp life and the all-male environment. Often guests brought homemade food, which was highly prized.

The young male CPSers all possessed keen appetites, so food and its preparation was a major unit activity. While each camp had a dietitian who supervised the food service, the men did the actual work. Since wartime food costs were high, and some food was

*This truck from Harper, Kansas, is arriving at a CPS camp with food from Mennonite communities.*

rationed, getting adequate supplies at reasonable cost was a major challenge for camp directors. Many camps had gardens where large quantities of vegetables were grown. The Mennonites set up a systematic CPS canning program whereby congregations canned food for specific camps, with MCC supplying the cans and labels, and transporting and distributing the goods. In 1944 CPS camps received 234,126 quarts of food valued at forty-three thousand dollars.

Base camps shared many common features. The CCC barracks set in isolated splendor offered few amenities. During the day when the men were on project only a few people were in evidence around the camps. So-called overhead men would be doing their chores — preparing food, doing the laundry, loading the truck with garbage, working on camp repair. Typewriters would be busy in the office as reports and correspondence were prepared. In large units, personnel issues such as furloughs, transfers and releases took up a lot of administrative time.

# 8

# The Price of Conscience

General Lewis Hershey enjoyed talking about CPS as a noble experiment in democracy, testing whether the United States could honor the conscience of a minority who rejected military service in wartime. But he always understood CPS as a privilege rather than a legal right. Hence, it was easy for him to ignore the constitutional problem posed by Congress' failure to provide compensation for CPS service. Many CPS men believed they were victims of involuntary servitude. The absence of compensation was especially galling when it became known that German prisoners of war received 80 cents a day for their labor.

Norman Thomas, leader of the Socialist party, challenged President Roosevelt on the matter but the President was unconvinced, arguing that the "needs of the Government are paramount to the desires of the individual."

Among those most victimized by this situation were the dependents of COs. Over one-third of all men in CPS were responsible for dependents. The pressure on many of them was inordinate. The Peace Churches tried to meet the needs as best they could. The Brethren, Friends and Mennonites provided $25 a month for each needy wife and $10 for each child. The National Service Board created a dependency fund for cases not covered by the Peace Churches. Their total fund was only $650 per month.

Had allotments been equal to servicemen's wives the total receipts from the government would have been two million dollars annually. Only about 5% of all CPS men received assistance for their dependents. It is estimated that during the life of CPS about a quarter million dollars was expended by the HPCs for dependents.

Aganetha Fast visited many CPS camps in the course of the War and was especially affected by the hardships many of the families of CPS men experienced as they sought to be near their loved ones. She wrote:

> In nearly all of the camps and units, I have found also quite a few of the CPS men's wives. They numbered from 15 to 55 per camp.

L. J. Anderson
400 Main Street
Placerville, CA

Dec. 29, 1942

Director Conscientious
Objectors Camp,
Camino, California

Dear Sir:

*I wish to enter a most strenuous protest against the action of some of the inmates of your camp by their intrusion at my home on Christmas Eve. Their presence was uninvited and certainly not wanted nor enjoyed. My family, consisting of a daughter in defense work, a son in the Navy, a daughter with two babies waiting for word from her husband missing on Bataan and my wife who is going thru a second war as a mother, were united for the first time since last summer and our Xmas was spoiled by this intrusion of your inmates. I will not be responsible if they come again.*

*I also wish to protest the action of the inmates in sending Xmas presents to the Japanese Camp at Poston Arizona. This interest shown in our enemies indicates sympathy for them which is decidedly un-American.*

They had left homes and home environment to be near their husbands. As they move close to the camp they live in primitive homes and surroundings . . . In most cases I found them living in only one tiny room: on the third story, in a dark basement, a barn or in tourist cabins. Most of the wives are working. They now serve in grocery stores, laundries, in dentists' offices, in restaurants and hotels as cooks, waitresses and maids, and in private homes as maids and housekeepers.

In 1943 Paul French proposed that the "frozen fund" be used to support dependents. The "frozen fund" had accumulated from the earnings of CPS men in detached service positions where they received compensation for their work. For instance, in mental hospitals the men received regular wages. After medical and insurance fees were paid, the men received $15 allowance per month, and the rest of their earnings were transferred to the Federal Treasury. The money could only be spent at the pleasure of the Congress.

In 1943 French, with the support of Selective Service, asked Congress to release the money for CPS dependents. The Bill found an unlikely defender in Senator John Sparkman of Alabama who argued, "this means, in effect, that we are penalizing wives and children because we do not agree with their husbands and fathers. Let us apply the restrictions to the men, if we will, but we should not extend the punishment to their families." The Bill failed.

Congress was more hawkish than the country. In a 1945 survey by Princeton Professor Leo Crespi on public attitudes toward COs he found that three-fourths of the American people believed that COs should receive wages and dependency allowances. Four-fifths endorsed the principle of alternative service for COs.

Many CPS men would have found the survey results hard to believe, for they experienced a lot of hostility from their fellow citizens. Quaker CPSer Thomas Waring tells of his trip to town for a pair of shoes while at Coleville, California (#37).

As he got off the Forestry Service truck he observed three local men sitting on a bench on the sidewalk. "One of them looked right at me and spat! The tobacco juice landed on my feet. I moved away, feeling their hostile gazes on my back. Goose bumps again. I hadn't had that feeling for six weeks."

He turned into the shoe store and as he opened the door a voice bellowed, " 'Get the hell out of here!' Stunned, he stood for a moment looking for the speaker. There was the owner of the store, balding, wearing red suspenders over a dirty undershirt, leaning on the counter. 'You heard me. We don't serve the likes of you in here. Now get out before I . . .' "

Waring left the store in a hurry. Hungry, he headed for the only diner in town. Before he got to the door the owner appeared with, "If you think I am going to serve you at my counter, you'd better think again. My advice is to get out of town. NOW!" Waring took his advice.

Sitting on the berm of the road outside of town, he mused, "It feels as if I were a Negro, or an American Indian, for that matter." A bit later a pickup truck pulled up and the friendly face of a rancher peered out at him. "Wanna ride, buddy? Goin' as far as Route 17. Where you headed?"

"I'm going to Coleville."

"You aren't one of those damn Conchies up there, are you?"

The man's face went dark and he drove off with his tires screeching.

Mervin Hostetler, who was at Mulberry, Florida (CPS #27), tells of meeting a slightly drunk man while walking through a rail underpass in town. The man grabbed him and threatened to beat him up for being a "conchie." Luckily a CPS buddy appeared. The man, startled, scrambled up to the railroad tracks where he met a black man, whom he gave a bear hug, shouting, "I'd rather hug a nigger [sic] than a filthy conchie!"

There were also many positive relationships. In April 1943 the CPS men at Denison, Iowa (CPS #18), helped build sandbag levees to control a flooding Missouri River at Council Bluffs. For ten days they worked side by side with hundreds of volunteers. Council Bluffs was extremely grateful and dispatched city engineer Jack Boyne to thank them. Boyne visited the 60 men at the Armory where they bunked.

"You've done a swell piece of work, boys," Boyne said. "How'd you like to go to a show?"

"We never go to shows," they said.

"Well!" Boyne countered, "can I send you some cigarettes?"

"We don't smoke," the conchies replied.

Boyne made a third attempt. "How about some beer then?"

"No!" they shouted, horrified.

"Isn't there anything I can do for you?" he asked.

"Yes," they said, "you can send us two new aprons for the cook and four dish towels." They were promptly provided.

## CPS—A Thriving, Unlikely Minority

During the years 1940 to 1945 more young male human beings were displaced than any time in human history. Tens of millions of young men lived in barracks, trenches and fields. It was an abnormal and brutal existence punctuated by fiery death and maiming. Few of those tens of millions could have received satisfaction from their

*I also protest the use of government trucks and tires for the private use of the inmates in making social contacts in this community. I call you to account as the Director of this camp because you assured me, when the camp was established, that there never would be any intrusion into the life of our community.*

*For your information I have written Gen. Hershey asking that the camp be removed from this community as a public menace and possible source of disturbance. We do not need the use of these inmates for the protection and production of our community.*

*Very truly yours,*

L. J. Anderson

*Camp Snowline*
*December 31, 1942*

*Dear Mr. Anderson:*
*We were quite surprised by your unexpected letter. In view of the facts presented in your letter we, unhesitatingly offer our sincere apologies. Our intention in singing the Christmas carols was to bring the Christmas Spirit with out necessarily making our identity known. Had we realized the situation would cause stress and strain we surely would not*

*have brought it about on the
Eve of the commemoration
of the birth of the Prince of
Peace.*

*We also would like to take
this opportunity to express
our sympathy with your
feelings for your son and
son-in-law. I, personally,
can do this whole-heartedly,
because I have an older
brother overseas somewhere
and a younger brother who
volunteered.*

*We trust that our apology
will be received in the same
spirit in which it is sent.*

*Sincerely,*
THE CAROL SINGERS

*Raymond L. Gorden*

*Chairman*

strange existence. And yet, obediently and often eagerly, they performed their bizarre duties.

The 12,000 CPS men and the 6,000 conscientious objectors in prison, combined with a few thousand British COs and a handful elsewhere in the world, were such a miniscule alternative to the warring tens of millions as to be nearly inexplicable. Why did that minority exist? What strage virus infected them? Or rather, what immunization protected them from the herd instincts of their fellows?

Few CPS men grasped the heroic quality of their alternative way at the time. Most made the choice out of their inherited identity with a tradition and community which stood at the center of their lives. Most believed that their most effective opposition to war was a kind of service which demonstrated an alternative to going to war. Consequently, they seldom found menial work in out-of-the-way places good enough. They wanted to do real service in settings of real need.

For some men the war required a more dramatic and decisive resistance. Altruistic service was too passive for these persons, its witness not sharp enough. Simple refusal to participate in war wasn't enough for them either. Their consciences required resistance to the war in a more overt form. Often these men became the "gadflies" in the camps, if they remained in the camps; more typically, they spent their time in prison.

The profound problem all COs faced was bound up in the service versus resistance arguments. Civilian Public Service was more altruistic service than overt resistance to war. One might argue it should have been more heavily tilted toward resistance. But that would have required a quite different system of Civilian Public Service. Whether a more war-resistant organization could have been possible is very doubtful.

CPS was not an ideal program; in fact it was seriously flawed. CPS, by its very existence, acknowledged the legitimacy of conscription, something many pacifists do not accept. The provision for work without pay carried a kind of Soviet "Gulag" quality of involuntary servitude. And there was always the odor and irony of the Historic Peace Churches helping the military state manage its conscription system.

CPS had significant formative influences. Given the powerful precedents set by CPS during World War II, alternative service is now a normal provision for American conscientious objectors. CPS was also a school for future leaders of the Historic Peace Churches. It thrust young men into positions of public responsibility as they struggled to make the CPS system work. Those men became, subsequently, the leaders of their churches and the burgeoning religious organizations of the post-war era.

CPS was not an ideal program. But in the brutal world of the 1940s the 12,000 CPS men stand out as an astounding anomaly. The actual condition of their service or servitude becomes less important than their simple but eloquent refusal to harm their fellow men. They performed great service, yet the stewardship of their service was sometimes imperfect. Their real significance lies not in their work or the nature of their organizational arrangements. It lies in what they represented and in their refusal to participate in the madness that was World War II.

# A Wife's Story
## Rachel S. Fisher

It was July 16, 1942 and I stood on the platform at the train station in Iowa City, Iowa, waving good-bye to my husband who was leaving for base camp at Henry, Illinois. At that time it seemed that my world was falling apart. We had been married for six months and were living on Bob's parents' farm. D. J. Fisher, minister and bishop for many years, was at retirement age and he and Mother Fisher had moved to Kalona.

If we had lived in another county, Bob might have received a farm deferment. However, the Johnson County draft board was rather harsh with COs and deferments were seldom given. Bob's sister and brother, both single, moved to the farm and I went home to my parents in Wellman, taking along our few items of furniture.

After visiting Bob one weekend, I decided to move to Henry, a small town, and find work. Although I was trained for secretarial work, I took a job as maid for a well-to-do widow for five dollars per week. Mrs. Dauber was very good to me and Bob was allowed to come to the house for visits. When it no longer seemed safe for me to drive to the camp (the local residents were becoming more and more hostile toward the COs), Mrs. Dauber would go for Bob and bring him back to the house for a visit. On the way she asked him to lie low in the car so he wouldn't be noticed by the local residents.

Because of the hostile attitude of the town, the whole camp was moved after four months to Downey, Idaho. The trip was made by train and took several days and nights.

Again I went home to my parents to decide what to do next. Idaho seemed a long distance away and my mother-in-law reminded me that there were Indians out there! However, it wasn't long until Bob encouraged me to come to Pocatello, about forty miles north of Downey. I traveled by train with a friend of ours who was on his way to Reedley, California. At Ogden, Utah, I left the train and took a bus to Pocatello where I lived with Elma Wenger, a General Conference Mennonite who was teaching in the city. Her home was at Filer, Idaho. We got along very well and had many good times together.

I found work as secretary for the Mayor of Pocatello. He was also an attorney. During the forenoon we were located in the city offices, and during the afternoon we were in his law office. I was impressed with the many spittoons in the corridors, and also in the attorney's office beside his desk. One day a drunk man came into the outer office where I worked alone. He wanted to see the attorney who was with a client. When I said he would have to wait, he suddenly said, "Shay, you're pretty. I'm going to kissh you." He started coming around my desk and I ran into the attorney's office, so frightened that I forgot the spittoon beside his desk. The attorney came to my rescue, kept me from falling into the spittoon, and ordered the man to leave!

We observed our first wedding anniversary in Pocatello and spent our first Christmas there, away from our families. I remember Christmas Day as a very lonely day and I was a bit homesick. Bob was allowed a certain number of 12-hour leaves and one weekend a month and camp was 40 miles away! But living in Pocatello was a good experience. The climate was wonderful, I did a lot of walking, we attended several Mormon churches, and yes, there were Indians who came to town and roamed through the stores. It was also my first contact with a member of the General Conference Mennonite Church, and Elma and I both treasured the privilege of living together those several months.

After four months at Downey, Bob volunteered to go to Ypsilanti State Hospital, Ypsilanti, Michigan, as a member of the first CPS unit there. We knew this would be another new experience but we both were eager to go. I planned to find secretarial work in Ann Arbor nearby rather than work at the State Hospital.

We arrived at YSH on April 1, 1943 and were immediately put in separate buildings. Bob joined the group of 50 CPS men who lived in "A" building and I was given a small room in the basement of the married couples building. A couple dozen CPS wives lived in the basement and we soon became acquainted (most of us were in our early 20s). We each had a small room with a bed, table and chair. Our husbands were allowed to come and visit us but they had to sign in their time of arrival and time of departure. If they did not leave before midnight, the matron came and knocked on our doors and told them to leave!

When I discovered that these young wives were working at the hospital, I decided I would too. I was immediately assigned to the business office where I worked until the Personnel Manager took a maternity leave. Then I was asked to serve as interim personnel manager for three months. This meant that I worked with all persons who applied for work at the hospital, taking counsel with the various supervisors and getting final ap-

proval from Dr. Yoder, the medical director. I was in and out of his office almost daily and we became friends. His secretary, whom he later married after his wife died, and I still keep in touch at Christmas time. Serving in this position was an excellent opportunity for me to learn to know hospital personnel and I found it very enjoyable.

After the personnel manager returned to her position, I was transferred to the Medical Stenographers Office. This again was a very interesting place to work. Each of us was assigned to a doctor or two and to one of the social workers. The doctors worked with the patients and the social workers with the family members. It was our responsibility to transcribe their dictation and enter it into each patient's file. Reading a patient's file gave me a new awareness of the fine line between mental health and mental illness.

Relationships between the "regular" employees and our group went well and so, after a number of months, Dr. Yoder decided that we could live together as couples. It was a happy day for all of us when our husbands joined us in the basement and we were given two small rooms which we made into a bedroom and a living room.

Besides the 50 men in the CPS unit there were about 25 wives employed at the hospital, and during the summer months another 25 single women joined the group and found employment. On Sunday evening we gathered for worship services. We had lots of good music and often a visiting speaker from a Mennonite church. Pastor Phil Frey and his wife from Archbold, Ohio, seemed to adopt our unit and often came to visit us.

During our three years at Ypsilanti State Hospital we had many interesting experiences: learning to know and love and work with General Conference Mennonites, taking classes in preparation for MCC relief work, playing tennis, riding bikes, owning a motorcycle, hitchhiking to Pigeon, Michigan, and to Cleveland, Ohio, to visit Bob's sisters, joining in worship services, visiting the small congregation at Pinckney, Michigan, and the Detroit Mission where the Rabers served.

Bob received his discharge papers from the U.S. government at the end of March, 1946. It was almost four years since we had left the farm and our home community. But before we went back to the farm we wanted to volunteer for a two-year term with MCC and this was done in Belgium and Poland. We shall always be grateful for the experiences we had living and working in Europe from 1946–1948, distributing food and clothing to those who suffered during the war. We also had the privilege of learning to know some of the Mennonites who were still living in Poland. If Bob had not been drafted in 1942 I doubt if we would have ever gone into relief work.

Our lives were truly blessed by our experiences during CPS.

# Map of CPS Camp Sites

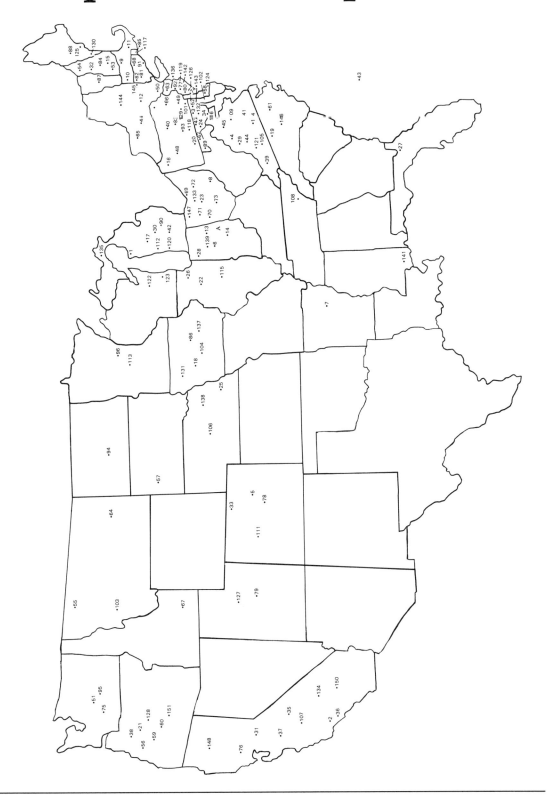

# Civilian Public Service Camps

| No. | Tech. Agency | Operat. Group | Location | Open. Date | Clos. Date |
|---|---|---|---|---|---|
| A | SCS | AFSC | Richmond, Ind. | June '41 | July '41 |
| 1 | FS | BSC | Manistee, Mich. | June '41 | July '41 |
| 2 | FS | AFSC | San Dimas, Calif. | June '41 | Dec. '42 |
| 3 | NPS | AFSC | Patapsco, Md. | May '41 | Sept. '42 |
| 4 | SCS | MCC | Grottoes, Va. | May '41 | May '46 |
| 5 | SCS | MCC | Colorado Springs, Colo. | June '41 | May '46 |
| 6 | SCS | BSC | Lagro, Ind. | May '41 | Nov. '44 |
| 7 | SCS | BSC | Magnolia, Ark. | June '41 | Nov. '44 |
| 8 | FS | MCC | Marietta, Ohio | June '41 | Apr. '43 |
| 9 | FS | AFSC | Petersham, Mass. | June '41 | Oct. '42 |
| 10 | FS | AFSC | Royalston, Mass. | June '41 | Oct. '42 |
| 11 | FS | AFSC | Ashburnham, Mass. | June '41 | Oct. '42 |
| 12 | FS | AFSC | Cooperstown, N.Y. | June '41 | May '45 |
| 13 | FS | MCC | Bluffton, Ind. | June '41 | Mar. '42 |
| 14 | SCS | AFSC | Merom, Ind. | June '41 | Apr. '43 |
| 15 | FS | ACCO | Stoddard, N.H. | Aug. '41 | Oct. '42 |
| 16 | FS | BSC | Kane, Pa. | July '41 | Nov. '44 |
| 17 | FS | BSC | Stronach, Mich. | Aug. '41 | June '42 |
| 18 | SCS | MCC | Denison, Iowa | Aug. '41 | Sept. '46 |
| 19 | NPS | AFSC | Buck Creek, N.C. | Aug. '41 | May '43 |
| 20 | SCS | MCC | Wells Tannery, Pa. | Oct. '41 | Oct. '44 |
| 21 | FS | BSC | Cascade Locks, Ore. | Nov. '41 | July '46 |
| 22 | SCS | MCC | Henry, Ill. | Nov. '41 | Nov. '42 |
| 23 | SCS | AFSC | Coshocton, Ohio | Jan. '42 | Feb. '46 |
| 24 | SCS | MCC | (1) Hagerstown, Md. | Feb. '42 | Sept. '46 |
|  |  | BSC | (2) Williamsport, Md. |  |  |
|  |  | MCC | (3) Boonsboro, Md. |  |  |
|  |  | MCC | (4) Clearspring, Md. |  |  |
|  |  | BSC | (5) New Windsor, Md. |  |  |
| 25 | SCS | MCC | Weeping Water, Nebr. | Apr. '42 | Apr. '43 |
| 26 | GH | ACCO | Chicago, Ill. | Mar. '42 | July '46 |
| 27 | PHS | BSC | (1) Tallahassee, Fla. | Mar. '42 |  |
|  |  | MCC | (2) Mulberry, Fla. & Bartow, Fla. |  | Dec. '46 |
|  |  | AFSC | (3) Orlando, Fla. |  |  |
|  |  | BSC | (4) Gainesville, Fla. |  |  |
| 28 | FS | MCC | Medaryville, Ind. | Apr. '42 | May '46 |
| 29 | FS | BSC | Lyndhurst, Va. | May '42 | Jan. '44 |
| 30 | FS | BSC | Walhalla, Mich. | May '42 | Nov. '43 |
| 31 | FS | MCC | Camino, Calif. | Apr. '42 | Dec. '46 |
| 32 | FS | AFSC | Campton, N.H. | May '42 | Nov. '43 |
| 33 | SCS | MCC | Fort Collins, Colo. Buckingham Side Camp | June '42 | Oct. '46 |
| 34 | F&W | *BSC | Bowie, Md. | June '42 |  |
| 34-D.S. |  |  | Detached Service |  |  |
| 35 | FS | MCC | North Fork, Calif. | May '42 | Mar. '46 |
| 36 | FS | BSC | Santa Barbara, Calif. | June'42 | Apr. '44 |

| No. | Tech. Agency | Operat. Group | Location | Open. Date | Clos. Date |
|---|---|---|---|---|---|
| 37 | FS | *AFSC | Coleville, Calif. | June '42 | Mar. '46 |
| 38 | Hosp. | BSC | Salem, Ore. | Not opened | |
| 39 | NPS | MCC | Galax, Va. | June '42 | Mar. '43 |
| 40 | SCS | MCC | Howard, Pa. | June '42 | June '43 |
| 41 | MH | *AFSC | Williamsburg, Va. | June '42 | July '46 |
| 42 | FS | BSC | Wellston, Mich. | June '42 | Sept. '46 |
| 43 | PRRA | BSC | Castaner Project Adjuntas, Puerto Rico | July '42 | |
| | | MCC | Aibonita, P.R. | | |
| | | AFSC | Zalduondo, P.R. | | |
| | | BSC | St. Thomas, Virgin Islands | | |
| 44 | MH | MCC | Staunton, Va | Aug. '42 | Sept. '46 |
| 45 | NPS | MCC | Luray, Va. | Aug. '42 | July '46 |
| 46 | SCS | *AFSC | Big Flats, N.Y. | Aug. '42 | Oct. '46 |
| 47 | MH | BSC | Sykesville, Md. | Aug. '42 | July '46 |
| 48 | FS | BSC | Marienville, Pa. | Oct. '42 | Nov. '43 |
| 49 | MH | *AFSC | Philadelphia, Pa. | Aug. '42 | Oct. '46 |
| 50 | MH | AFSC | New York, N.Y. | Sept. '42 | Jan. '46 |
| 51 | MH | BSC | Ft. Steilacoom, Wash. | Sept. '42 | Oct. '45 |
| 52 | SCS | AFSC-MCC | Powellsville, Md. | Oct. '42 | |
| 53 | FS | AFSC | Gorham, N.H. | Oct. '42 | Apr. '43 |
| 54 | FS | ACCO | Warner, N.H. | Oct. '42 | Feb. '43 |
| 55 | NPS | MCC | Belton, Mont. | Sept. '42 | Oct. '46 |
| 56 | FS | BSC | Waldport, Ore. | Oct. '42 | Apr. '46 |
| 57 | BR | MCC | Hill City, S. Dak. | Oct. '42 | May '46 |
| 58 | MH | MCC | Farnhurst, Dela. | Nov. '42 | Oct. '46 |
| 59 | GLO | AFSC | Elkton, Ore. | Nov. '42 | Feb. '46 |
| 60 | BR | MCC | Lapine, Ore. | Dec. '42 | Jan. '43 |
| 61 | GH | MCWP | Durham, N.C. | Dec. '42 | Oct. '46 |
| 62 | TS | *AFSC | Cheltenham, Md. | Dec. '42 | Apr. '46 |
| 63 | MH | MCC | Marlboro, N.J. | Nov. '42 | Oct. '46 |
| 64 | FSA | MCC | Terry, Mont. | Jan. '43 | July '46 |
| 65 | MH | | Utica, N.Y. | Not opened | |
| 66 | MH | MCC | Norristown, Pa | Dec. '42 | Oct. '46 |
| 67 | SCS | MCC | Downey, Idaho | Nov. '42 | Feb. '46 |
| 68 | MH | BSC | Norwich, Conn. | Mar. '43 | Aug. '46 |
| 69 | MH | AFSC-MCC | Cleveland, Ohio | Dec. '42 | Oct. '46 |
| 70 | MH | BSC | Dayton, Ohio | Oct. '43 | June '46 |
| 71 | MH | MCC | Lima, Ohio | Jan. '43 | Sept. '46 |
| 72 | MH | MCC | Macedonia, Ohio | Dec. '42 | Sept. '46 |
| 73 | MH | BSC | Columbus, Ohio | Dec. '42 | June '46 |
| 74 | MH | BSC | Cambridge, Md. | Dec. '42 | July '46 |
| 75 | MH | AFSC | Medical Lake, Wash. | Feb. '43 | May '45 |
| 76 | FS | *AFSC | Glendora, Calif. | Jan. '43 | Dec. '46 |
| 77 | MH | MCC | Greystone Park, N.J. | Jan. '43 | Aug. '46 |
| 78 | MH | MCC | Denver, Colo. | Jan. '43 | Mar. '46 |
| 79 | MH | MCC | Provo, Utah | Mar. '43 | Apr. '46 |
| 80 | MH | BSC | Lyons, N.J. | Apr. '43 | Aug. '46 |
| 81 | MH | *AFSC | Middletown, Conn. | Mar. '43 | Sept. '46 |
| 82 | MH | BSC | Newtown, Conn. | Mar. '43 | Sept. '46 |
| 83 | MH | *AFSC | Warren, Pa. | Feb. '43 | May '46 |
| 84 | MH | *AFSC | Concord, N.H. | Feb. '43 | June '46 |
| 85 | MH | MCC | Howard, R.I. | Feb. '43 | Oct. '46 |
| 86 | MH | MCC | Mt. Pleasant, Iowa | Feb. '43 | Sept. '46 |

| No. | Tech. Agency | Operat. Group | Location | Open. Date | Clos. Date |
|---|---|---|---|---|---|
| 87 | MH | *AFSC | Brattleboro, Vt. | Feb. '43 | Sept. '46 |
| 88 | MH | BSC | Augusta, Maine | Apr. '43 | May '46 |
| 89 | FS | AFSC | Oakland, Md. | Mar. '43 | Apr. '43 |
| 90 | MH | MCC | Ypsilanti, Mich. | Mar. '43 | Oct. '46 |
| 91 | MH | BSC | Mansfield, Conn. | Mar. '43 | Aug. '46 |
| 92 | TS | MCC | Vineland, N.J. | Apr. '43 | June '46 |
| 93 | MH | MCC | Harrisburg, Pa. | Apr. '43 | Aug. '46 |
| 94 | FSA | *AFSC | Trenton, N. Dak. | Apr. '43 | Mar. '46 |
| 95 | TS | BSC | Buckley, Wash. | May '43 | Oct. '45 |
| 96 | MH | MCC | Rochester, Minn. | | |
| 97 | ALA | AFSC-BSC- | Dairy Farm and | | |
| & | | MCC | Dairy Herd Tester Proj. | May '43 | Oct. '46 |
| 100 | | (BSC) | Oneida, N.Y. | | |
| | | | King Co., Wash. | | |
| | | | Coos Co., Ore. | | |
| | | | Elgin, Ill. | | |
| | | | New Windsor, Md. | | |
| | | (MCC) | Colorado Area | | |
| | | | Penna. and Md. Area | | |
| | | | Mich. and Ohio Area | | |
| | | | New England Area | | |
| | | | Pacific Coast Area | | |
| | | | Wisconsin Area | | |
| | | | Iowa Area | | |
| | | | Maine Area | | |
| | | (AFSC) | Eastern Area | | |
| 98 | C&GS | SSS | Coast & Geodetic Survey | May '43 | Sept. '46 |
| 99 | FS&R | AFSC | Chungking, China | May '43 | Oct. '43 |
| 100 | (See No. 97) | | | | |
| 101 | DS | NSBRO | Foreign Relief & Rehabilitation Proj., Philadelphia, Pa. | May '43 | Oct. '43 |
| 102 | TS | *ACCO | Rosewood, Owings Mills, Md. | May '43 | July '46 |
| 103 | FS | MCC | Missoula, Mont. | May '43 | Apr. '46 |
| 104 | AES | *AFSC | Ames, Iowa | May '43 | May '46 |
| 105 | MH | BSC | Lynchburg, Colony, Va. | May '43 | Apr. '46 |
| 106 | AES | MCC | Lincoln — No. Platte, Nebr. | May '43 | Oct. '46 |
| 107 | NPS | MCC | Three Rivers, Calif. | May '43 | June '46 |
| 108 | NPS | *AFSC | Gatlinburg, Tennessee | June '43 | Dec. '46 |
| 109 | MH | BSC | Marion, Va. | June '43 | June '46 |
| 110 | MH | MCC | Allentown, Pa. | Nov. '43 | May '46 |
| 111 | BR | SSS | Mancos, Colo. | July '43 | Feb. '46 |
| 112 | AES | BSC | East Lansing, Mich. | July '43 | Apr. '46 |
| 113 | AES | BSC | Duluth, Grand Rapids, St. Paul & Waseca, Minn. | Aug. '43 | Aug. '46 |
| 114 | WB | BSC | Mt. Weather, Bluemont, Va. | Sept. '43 | June '46 |
| 115 | OSRD | AFSC-BSC-MCC | Office of Scientific Research & Development | Oct. '43 | Oct. '46 |
| 116 | AES | BSC | College Park, Md. | Sept. '43 | Sept. '46 |
| 117 | TS | MCC | Lafayette, R. I. | Nov. '43 | Aug. '46 |
| 118 | MH | MCC | Wernersville, Pa. | Nov. '43 | June '46 |
| 119 | TS | *AFSC | New Lisbon, N.J. | Dec. '43 | Oct. '46 |
| 120 | MH | MCC | Kalamazoo, Mich. | Dec. '43 | July '46 |
| 121 | NPS | BSC | Bedford, Va. | Feb. '44 | June '46 |
| 122 | MH | MCC | Winnebago, Wisc. | Dec. '43 | Mar. '46 |
| 123 | TS | MCC | Union Grove, Wisc. | Dec. '43 | July '46 |

| No. | Tech. Agency | Operat. Group | Location | Open. Date | Clos. Date |
|---|---|---|---|---|---|
| 124 | TS | *AFSC | Stockley, Dela. | Dec. '43 | Sept. '46 |
| 125 | AES | MCC | Orono, Maine | Dec. '43 | May '46 |
| 126 | USDA | MCC | Beltsville, Md. | Feb. '44 | Dec. '46 |
| 127 | TS | MCC | American Fork, Utah | Jan. '44 | Feb. '46 |
| 128 | BR | SSS | Lapine, Ore. | Jan. '44 | Dec. '46 |
| 129 | MH | *AFSC | Pennhurst, Spring City, Pa. | Jan. '44 | Aug. '46 |
| 130 | TS | *AFSC | Pownal, Maine | Feb. '44 | July '46 |
| 131 | MH | MCWP | Cherokee, Iowa | Feb. '44 | May '46 |
| 132 | TS | *AFSC | Laurel, Md. | Feb. '44 | July '46 |
| 133 | AES | *AFSC | Wooster, Ohio | Mar. '44 | Apr. '46 |
| 134 | FS | BSC | Belden, Calif. | May '44 | May '46 |
| 135 | F&W | SSS | Germfask, Mich. | May '44 | June '45 |
| 136 | MH | *ABHMS | Skillman, N.J. | July '44 | Oct. '46 |
| 137 | MH | Ev.&Ref. | Independence, Iowa | Dec. '44 | Sept. '46 |
| 138 | SCS | MCC | (1) Lincoln, Nebr.<br>(2) Malcolm, Nebr.<br>(3) Waterloo, Nebr. | Oct. '44 | Dec. '46 |
| 139 | MH | Disc. of Chr. | Logansport, Ind. | Oct. '44 | Apr. '46 |
| 140 | OSG | AFSC-BSC | Army Epidemiological Board | Feb. '45 | Oct. '46 |
| 141 | PHS | MCC | Gulfport, Miss. | Feb. '45 | Not closing |
| 142 | MH | MCC | Woodbine, N.J. | Jan. '45 | July '46 |
| 143 | MH | MCC | Catonsville, Md. | Feb. '45 | Aug. '46 |
| 144 | MH | MCC | Poughkeepsie, N.Y. | Apr. '45 | Apr. '46 |
| 145 | TS | MCC | Wassiac, N.Y. | | |
| 146 | AES | BSC | Ithaca, N.C. | July '45 | June '46 |
| 147 | MH | MCC | Tiffin, Ohio | June '45 | Nov. '45 |
| 148 | FS | SSS | Minersville, Calif. | June '45 | Dec. '46 |
| 149 | FS | AFSC-BSC | U.S. Forest Service Research Proj. | June '45 | June '46 |
| 150 | MH | MCC | Livermore, Calif. | Nov. '45 | Dec. '46 |
| 151 | MH | MCC | Roseburg, Ore. | Dec. '45 | Dec. '46 |

*Legend*

| | | | | |
|---|---|---|---|---|
| * | Taken over by Government before unit closed | | GH | General Hospital |
| | | | GLO | General Land Office |
| ABHMS | American Baptist Home Mission Society | | MCC | Mennonite Central Committee |
| ACCO | Association of Catholic Conscientious Objectors | | MCWP | Methodist Commission on World Peace |
| | | | MH | Mental Hospital |
| AES | Agriculture Experiment Station | | NPS | National Park Service |
| AFSC | American Friends Service Committee | | NSBRO | National Service Board for Religious Objectors |
| ALA | Agriculture Experiment Station | | | |
| BR | Bureau of Reclamation | | OSG | Office of Surgeon General |
| BSC | Brethren Service Committee | | OSBD | Office of Scientific Research & Development |
| C&GS | Coast & Goedetic Survey | | PHS | Public Health Service |
| Disc. Chr. | Disciples of Christ | | PRRA | Puerto Rican Reconstruction Administration |
| E&R | Evangelical & Reformed | | SCS | Soil Conservation Service |
| F&W | Fish & Wild Life | | SSS | Selective Service System |
| FS | Forest Service | | TS | Training School |
| FS&R | Foreign Service & Relief | | WB | Weather Bureau |
| FSA | Farm Security Administration | | | |

# A Gallery of Photos

*A group of CPSers enjoys a laugh in their bunkhouse.*

*Right: Noon lunch at a CPS camp.*
*Below: Group portrait of CPS #23 at Coshocton, Ohio (AFSC).*

*Above: CPS #27 in Mulberry, Florida, January 1944. Kneeling—Herman Ropp, George Bohrer, Arthur Thiessen, Ethan Horst, Jacob Guhr, Edwin Weaver, Ernest Miller. Standing—Ernest Pankratz, Harold Thiessen, William Yoder, Delmar Stahly, Dennis Lehman, Lester Hiebert, John Horst, M. C. Lehman, Wesley Prieb, Paul Schmidt, Galen Widmer, Menno Lohrenz, Willard Baer, Paul Miller, Roland Bartel, Ernest Shank, Franklin Wiebe, Roland Kauffman, Leo Goertz, Mrs. Harold Martin, Harold Martin, C. Nelson Hostetler.*

*Left: Personnel at a CPS camp in Powellsville, Maryland—Betty Mellor (dietician), Alice Beaman (nurse), Ruth Seegir (assistant director's wife).*

*Above: Colonel Kosch talks to a group of CPS men.*
*Below: Personnel at a CPS camp.*

*Left: Saying good-bye to a group of men in a Hagerstown, Maryland, camp, who are leaving for a new assignment.*

*Below: A Mennonite camp directors conference at CPS #18, in Denison, Iowa.*

*Right: A CPS camp meeting.
Below: COs hang out
laundry during a wash day
at the camp.*

*Left: Producing the camp paper at CPS #24, Hagerstown, Maryland.*

*Below: A group portrait of CPS #6 at Lagro, Indiana. Seated—Long, Fuson, Lockwood, Swan, Hertzler, Butcher, Weaver. Standing—Sollenberger, Nabel, Funke, Boag, Stanley, Phend, Kidder, Coffman.*

*Right:* A class of men studies the social roots of poverty at Hill City, South Dakota, CPS #57.

*Below:* The men at camp Magnolia, Arkansas, a Brethren Service camp (CPS #7).

*Left: CPS men moving dirt at CPS #18 in Denison, Iowa, an MCC camp.*
*Below: CPS #66 group picture at Norristown State Hospital.*

*Building forms for the concrete overflow structure in a dam near Denison, Iowa (CPS #18, MCC).*

*Left: Civilian Public Service personnel at a Powellsville, Maryland, camp. Below: CPS #20 in Wells Tannery, Pennsylvania.*

*Right: Administrative staff at CPS #8 in Marietta, Ohio, a Mennonite camp—David Wedel (director), Ruth Eschleman (nurse), Ruth Schmidt (nurse), Robert Eschleman (business manager).*

*Below: A group of AFSC personnel in an Orlando, Florida, camp.*

*Horseshoes was a popular recreation activity.*

*Right: Going to work at CPS #8 in Marietta, Ohio, a Mennonite camp.*

*Below: A group from CPS #20 planting trees in Wells Tannery, Pennsylvania.*

# Bibliography

Bowman, Rufus D. *The Church Of The Brethren And War, 1708–1941.* Elgin, Illinois: Brethren Publishing House, 1944.

*Directory of Civilian Public Service.* Washington: National Service Board for Religious Objectors, 1947.

Durnbaugh, Donald F. *To Serve The Present Age.* Elgin, Illinois: Brethren Press, 1975.

Durnbaugh, Donald F. *Pragmatic Prophet: The Life Of Michael Robert Zigler.* Elgin, Illinois: Brethren Press, 1989.

Eisan, Leslie. *Pathways to Peace.* Elgin, Illinois: Brethren Publishing House, 1948.

*The Experience of the American Friends Service Committee in Civilian Public Service.* Philadelphia: American Friends Service Committee, 1945.

Flynn, George Q. *Lewis B. Hershey, Mr. Selective Service.* Chapel Hill: University of North Carolina, 1985.

Gingerich, Melvin. *Service for Peace.* Akron, Pennsylvania: Mennonite Central Committee, 1949.

Keim, Albert, and Grant Stoltzfus. *The Politics of Conscience: The Historic Peace Churches and America at War, 1917–1955.* Scottdale, Pennsylvania: Herald Press, 1988.

Klippenstein, Lawrence, ed. *That There Be Peace: Mennonites in Canada and World War II.* Winnipeg, Manitoba: Conscientious Objectors Reunion Committee, 1979.

Olmstead, Frank. *They Asked For A Hard Job: COs At Work In Mental Hospitals.* New York. Plowshare Press, 1943.

Pickett, Clarence. *For More Than Bread.* Boston: Little, Brown and Co., 1953.

Sibly, Mulford Q. and Philip E. Jacob. *Conscription of Conscience: The American State And The Conscientious Objector, 1940–1947.* Ithaca: Cornell University Press, 1952.

Wagler, David and Roman Raber. *The Story Of The Amish In Civilian Public Service.* North Newton, Kansas: Bethel Press, 1945.

Waring, Thomas. *Something For Peace: A Memoir.* Hanover, New Hampshire: 1989.

Wittner, Lawrence S. *Rebels Against War.* New York: Columbia University Press, 1969.

Wright, Frank, Jr. *Out Of Sight, Out Of Mind.* Philadelphia: National Mental Health Foundation, 1947.

Zahn, Gordon. *Another Part Of The War: The Camp Simon Story.* Amherst, Massachussetts: University of Mass. Press, 1979.

# About the Author

The author has one personal memory of CPS. In 1943, when he was eight years old, his Amish parents and a brother and sister traveled by train from Hartville, Ohio, to Lancaster, Pennsylvania, to visit relatives. Sometime during the journey they took a side trip to visit a young neighbor who was in CPS at Norristown State Hospital. Keim still remembers the terror he felt as they were ushered through the wards.

Albert Keim was drafted in 1955 and spent two years as a conscientious objector, working for the Mennonite Central Committee PAX service in Germany. As for so many CPS men, Keim found this stint in alternative service to be a life-changing experience, which led, among other things, to education, culminating in his receiving a Ph.D. in history from Ohio State University.

The author has been a teacher at Eastern Mennonite College since 1965. His field of study is recent American history. His specialty is religion and public policy issues. In 1975 he published **Compulsory Education and the Amish** (Beacon Press), and in 1988 **The Politics of Conscience: the Historic Peace Churches and War, 1917–1955** (Herald Press).

The author's wife, Leanna Yoder Keim, is a self-employed potter and teaches part-time in the art department of Eastern Mennonite Col-

lege. The Keims are the parents of one daughter and became grandparents for the first time this summer. The Keims are members of the Park View Mennonite congregation in Harrisonburg, Virginia.